Augustus Franks

**Japanese pottery**

Being a native report

Augustus Franks

**Japanese pottery**
*Being a native report*

ISBN/EAN: 9783337174910

Printed in Europe, USA, Canada, Australia, Japan

Cover: Foto ©Andreas Hilbeck / pixelio.de

More available books at **www.hansebooks.com**

# JAPANESE POTTERY

BEING A NATIVE REPORT

WITH AN INTRODUCTION AND CATALOGUE

BY

AUGUSTUS W. FRANKS, M.A., F.R.S., F.S.A.

WITH ILLUSTRATIONS AND MARKS

*Published for the Committee of Council on Education*

BY

CHAPMAN AND HALL, Limited, 193, PICCADILLY.

1880

CHARLES DICKENS AND EVANS,
CRYSTAL PALACE PRESS.

# CONTENTS.

## CONTENTS.

# LIST OF ILLUSTRATIONS.

# PREFACE.

*IT may be well to say a few words as to the origin and scope of this publication, and to explain why it differs somewhat from an ordinary handbook.*

*While preparations were being made for the Philadelphia Exhibition, it occurred to the authorities of the South Kensington Museum that it would be an interesting feature in the Japanese Section of that Exhibition if a representative series of the older Japanese Ceramic wares were to form part of it.*

*The Japanese authorities readily entered into the proposed arrangement, and much credit is due to them for the admirable manner in which this interesting collection was made, within a limit of price, by obtaining from the various parts of the Japanese Empire specimens of interest. It was arranged that after the Exhibition the collection should become the property of the South Kensington Museum. This arrangement was facilitated by Mr. Fritz Cunliffe-Owen, at that time in the Japanese service, and residing in Tokio, and a Report on*

*Japanese Ceramics was prepared by Mr. M. Shioda, and translated by Mr. T. Asami, to accompany and illustrate the collection.*

*This Report forms the most important portion of the present volume; the only alterations that have been made in editing it are to bring the Japanese names to a uniform and accepted mode of spelling, and to correct the phraseology so as to make the meaning of the writer more clear. In doing this I have had the assistance of my Japanese friends Mr. B. Nanjio and Mr. K. Kasawara, and to these gentlemen I am indebted for much other help. A short list of the specimens accompanied the collection, which has furnished most of the dates. As it seemed indispensable, in order that the Report might be made intelligible and useful, that the specimens themselves should be fully described, a new catalogue has been made of them.*

*The other Japanese specimens in the Museum might have been included, but this would have destroyed the value of the collection as a representative series according to Japanese views, and it would have been difficult in all cases to classify objects gathered from so many different sources.*

*Mr. Ninagawa of Tokio has published a work on Japanese pottery, entitled " Kwan ko dzu setsu," in five parts, with illustrations, and a translation of the text has appeared in French. This work has been made use of to a certain extent in the Introduction and notes, but in a less degree than I should have wished, as the accuracy of the French translation seems doubtful, the author being unacquainted with the language into which his work was translated, and the translator evidently unfamiliar with the technical terms. The additions to the Report are indicated by square brackets.*

*The only other work on Japanese pottery that need be mentioned is "The Keramic Art of Japan," of Messrs. Audsley and Bowes, now completed, in which will be found illustrations of the more ornate specimens of Japanese wares.*

*It is scarcely necessary to allude to the works of the distinguished writer M. Jacquemart, as I differ entirely from him with regard to most of the porcelain which he has attributed to Japan. His Corean porcelain is old Japanese, his Chinese "chrysanthémo-pæonienne" ware is likewise Japanese, somewhat later in date, while his Japanese eggshell and mandarin vases are unquestionably Chinese. Excellent illustrations of Japanese vases may be found in his books, from the hand of that talented artist M. Jules Jacquemart.*

*I have thought it of interest to add, as an Appendix, a list of the potters and factories that exhibited at the Universal Exhibition at Paris in 1878, more especially as by the kind help of Mr. Kawara, my Japanese colleague on the Ceramic Jury, and his obliging associate M. Suoda, I was enabled to obtain the names of the Japanese potters in full and to eliminate mere exhibitors.*

*I must add that, in preparing this work I have been much assisted by my private secretary, Mr. Charles H. Read, who has in great measure made the catalogue of the specimens forming the collection, and has copied with accuracy the marks which it has been thought desirable to engrave in facsimile. He has also assisted me in other sections of the work.*

*AUGUSTUS W. FRANKS.*

*British Museum,*
    *June,* 1880.

# INTRODUCTION

THE great admiration that has long been felt in Europe for Japanese porcelain, and the further interest recently awakened, since the opening of the ports, by the still more original earthenware of that country, render it necessary to make some observations on the history and ornamentation of this branch of decorative art.

Before doing so, however, we must consider some national peculiarities and customs which have had great influence on the arts of Japan, and especially on its pottery.

The Japanese, unlike the Chinese, and beyond all Oriental nations, have allowed themselves to be subject to foreign influence. Most of their arts and sciences, their language, writing, and literature, and even one of their principal religions, they have derived from other countries, and in a great measure from the Chinese continent, either from China itself or from Corea. Though, however, they are so much indebted to other lands, they have imparted to the borrowed style a charm of its own, due to their native originality, and fostered by powerful and wealthy nobles, a class scarcely existing in China.

As will be seen in the Report, the Japanese trace several of their improvements to the teaching of Corean potters, who seem to have settled in the country at various times, ranging over a

B

long period, from B.C. 27 to the end of the seventeenth century of our era.*

Although, however, the Coreans may have been able to teach the Japanese some of the elementary processes, yet as all the specimens we have seen of Corean work are very rude and unshapely, it is probable that this constant importation of Corean potters was in a great measure due to another cause, to which we shall have occasion presently to allude.

It is to the Chinese that they are really indebted for their greatest advances. The first good Japanese glazed pottery was made at Seto, about 1230, by Tôshiro, who had learnt the art in China, whence he even brought some of his materials. The first porcelain made in Japan is attributed to Gorodayu Shonsui, who returned from China about 1513. The only pottery of a superior kind which claims a Corean origin is the well-known Satsuma ware; but the earlier specimens of that ware are no better than the contemporary Japanese productions, and it is a question whether the superior merits of that pottery are not due to the influence of Japanese taste, and to the patronage of the powerful princes of Satsuma. The finer specimens, at any rate, of that factory were made long after the Coreans were first established there.

The fondness of the Japanese for foreign wares is shown by the relative values placed by their collectors on different kinds of pottery. First comes pottery made in Corea itself; secondly, very ancient Japanese pottery; thirdly, Chinese porcelain, especially of single colours; their own porcelain they do not seem to collect to the same extent. In fact the Japanese collector, where pottery and porcelain are concerned, cares little for high finish or elaborate ornament ; a rough, sketchy, but picturesque design is far more pleasing to him than the elegant forms and rich decoration which we are accustomed to hold in esteem.

* See Catalogue of the Franks Collection exhibited at Bethnal Green, 2nd ed. p. 141.

This explains the notable fact that in none of the collections, formed before the opening of Japan to Western commerce in 1859, do we find any specimens of Japanese pottery, and rarely more than one class of Japanese porcelain, a class made almost entirely for exportation, and which we know as " Old Japan." The real reason, however, why the Japanese attach such a fanciful value to Corean vessels, and why they imported Corean potters long after they themselves had made so much progress in the art, is due to the Tea Ceremonies ; and it may be well to give a slight sketch of the nature of these peculiar institutions.

The Tea Ceremonies, known as the " Cha-no-yu," do not appear to have been noticed at any length in any English work, though a short account of them, obtained from Baron Alexander von Siebold, may be found in the English translation of Dr. Jagor's " Travels in the Philippines " (p. 167). A much fuller description of them has been published by Dr. Funk, in the sixth part of the "Mittheilungen der deutschen Gesellschaft für Natur und Völkerkunde Ostasiens," Yokohama, 1874, from which our account of them has been condensed, with some additional information kindly furnished by Mr. Kasawara.

The cultivation of tea is said to have been introduced into Japan from China in A.D. 805, though it did not take firm hold till later.

It is uncertain when the tea ceremonies or clubs first commenced ; and they do not appear to have adopted fixed rules till the middle of the fifteenth century. These rules were made by a Japanese named Shuko, under the patronage of the Shogun Yosimasa (1443 — 1473); later the famous Taiko Hideyosi appointed another Japanese, named Rikiu, to revise the old statutes, and the rules drawn up by him are still observed.

There are, or rather were, several varieties in the observance of the ceremonies, of which the principal are Senké, Enshu, Oribé, Matsu-o, and Yabu-no-uchi. Under the present régime they are nothing more than friendly réunions ; the ceremonies in fact are dying out, and will probably have entirely disappeared in a few years.

The place destined for the ceremonies is either a separate building, or an apartment removed from the rest of the house, and it was known under the names of *Kakoi* (the enclosed), or *Sukiya.* It was covered with shingles, and consisted of a room usually measuring 4½ mats (a mat = about 6 by 3 feet), or, about 81 square feet; on one side was another smaller room, called *Midzu-ya* (water-room), where the utensils were arranged; on the other side was another small room for receiving the guests. Surrounding the house or apartment was a garden, *Ro-ji* (dewy ground).

Two modes of conducting the ceremonies were observed—the winter and summer modes. In the former the garden was strewn with fir leaves, the guests retained their shoes, and the furnace for the kettle was a pit in the floor filled with ashes. In the latter, the garden was decked out with flowers, the guests took off their shoes, and a portable earthenware furnace (*furo*) was used.

The inside of the room was to be as plain as possible, though costly woods might be employed if the means of the host admitted it. The walls had a dado of white paper, and on one side was a niche (*toko*), with an inscribed roll and flowers, the latter sometimes placed in a hanging vase. The hours fixed for the invitations were 4 to 6 A.M., noon, or 6 P.M. The guests, assembling in a pavilion (*machi ai*) in the garden, announce their arrival by striking on a wooden tablet (*han*) or bell, when the host himself or a servant appears to conduct them into the chamber. The entrance being only three feet square, the host kneels and lets the guests creep in before him. They being seated in a semicircle, the host goes to the door of the side room in which the utensils are kept, saying : " I am very glad that you are come, and thank you much. I now go to make up the fire." He then brings in a basket (*sumi-tori*) containing charcoal in pieces of a prescribed length, a brush (*mitsu-ba*) made of three feathers, a pair of tongs (*hibashi*), the stand of the kettle (*kama-shiki*), iron handles for the kettle, a lacquer box* containing incense† (*kobako*), and some paper. He again leaves the chamber to bring in a vessel with ashes (*hai-ki*) (see Nos. 74 to 77) and its spoon. He then makes up the fire and burns incense, to overpower the smell of the charcoal. While he is thus occupied, the guests beg to be allowed to inspect the incense-box, generally an object of value, which passes from hand to hand, and the last guest returns it to the host. This closes the first part of the ceremony, and both host and guests withdraw.

The second part commences with eating, and, as it is a rule that nothing should be left, the guests carry off, wrapped up in paper, any fragments that remain. The utensils used in this part of the ceremony are as follows :

1. An iron kettle (*kama*) with a copper or iron lid, resting on a stand (*kama-shiki*).

2. A table or stand (*daisu*) of mulberry wood, two feet high.

3. Two tea jars (*cha-ire*) containing the fine powdered tea, and enclosed in bags of brocade.

4. A vessel containing fresh water (*midzu-sashi*), which is placed under the *daisu*.

5. A tea bowl of porcelain or earthenware (*cha-wan*, or, when of large size, *temmoku*), simple in form, but remarkable for its antiquity or historical associations.

Besides these there is a bamboo whisk (*cha-sen*); a silk cloth (*fukusa*), usually purple, for wiping the utensils; a spoon (*cha-shaku*) to take the tea out of the *cha-ire*; and a water ladle (*shaku*). All these objects are brought in singly by the host in their prescribed order.‡

After solemn salutations and obeisances the utensils are wiped

---

* This is used in the summer mode. In the winter a porcelain or earthenware box (*kogo*) is employed.

† In the winter odoriferous pastilles are burned, in the summer sandal wood.

‡ The woodcut on the next page represents a bamboo whisk and a spoon belonging to a tea apparatus in the Christy Collection.

and some of the powdered tea is placed in the tea bowl, hot water is poured on it, and the whole is vigorously stirred with the whisk until it looks like thin spinach ; a boy then carries the bowl to the chief guest, from whom it passes round the party to the last, who returns it empty to the boy. The empty bowl is then passed round once more that the guests may admire it. The utensils are then washed by the host, and the ceremony is at an end.

The rules forbid any conversation on worldly subjects, such as politics or scandal ; flattery is also forbidden, and, properly speaking, the meeting should not last longer than two hours.. No distinction of ranks is observed.

There can, however, be no doubt that in early times these

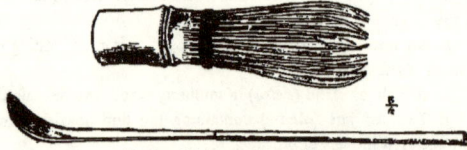

Bamboo Whisk and Jointed Spoon.

societies were encouraged by the princes, that their retainers might have an opportunity of quietly promoting the political designs of their lords.

The ceremonial described above is that known as the "Koi-cha," and Dr. Funk states that he was present on one of these occasions when the tea bowl and water jar were exhibited with much pride as old Corean ; the host dilated on the age and origin of the various utensils, and mentioned, for instance, that the bag of one of the tea jars was made from the dress of the celebrated dancer Kogaru, who lived in the time of Taiko Hideyosi.

There is another form of the tea ceremonies, the "Usu-cha" (weak tea), which differs from the first in some respects. It is far less ceremonious, the tea is thinner and of inferior quality, and the bowl is filled afresh for each guest, being rinsed out with water each time. The tea jar is also different, being a *natsumé* made of lacquer.

The tea used in both these ceremonies comes from Uji, near Kiôto, the most celebrated tea district of Japan, and is differently prepared from the commencement according to the ceremony for which it is intended.

These ceremonies were the cause of the large prices occasionally paid for the vessels of pottery used in them, especially while they were in the height of fashion, hence we hear that, in the time of Taiko Hideyosi, a single tea bowl of Seto ware was sold for some thousand dollars (see p. 29).

### HISTORY.

We must now consider somewhat more in detail the history of the Ceramic art in Japan.

It will be seen that the Japanese writers refer the origin of the making of pottery to a remote period, anterior to B.C. 660, their date for the commencement of real history in Japan, and a specimen considered to be of this period is to be found in the collection (No. 1). The date assigned to it must of course be purely conjectural. Such vases are found in ancient tombs, and from their sometimes containing claw-like ornaments in hard stone, they are known as *magatama tsubo,* or "precious jewel vases." They are probably the remains of a race which preceded the existing Japanese, though perhaps to a certain extent merged in it—a race connected with the Ainos, and who are known to have occupied, even in historic times, the northern part of the main island. It will be seen that the pottery is coarsely made, and resembles somewhat the early pottery of Europe. Some of the specimens, however, have a considerable affinity to vessels discovered in North America, the exact age of which is not settled.

During the first two centuries of our era Corean potters came to Japan, and no doubt introduced some improvements; one of the greatest, however, was due to native talent, being the introduction of the potters' wheel by Giyogi, a native of the province of Idzumi, by whom the flask No. 2 is said to have been made. To revert to the Coreans—it must be remembered that the peninsula of Corea, projecting as it does from the north-east of China towards the Japanese islands, has been the route by which many of the arts and sciences have travelled to the latter country, though perhaps originating still farther to the west. It was anciently divided into three kingdoms, Kaoli, Petsi, and Sinra, which were united into one about the middle of the tenth century. Its peculiar position brought upon it a limited subjection to both China and Japan, varying from time to time, and never well defined.

In the early part of the reign of the Emperor Suinin, B.C. 27, the followers of the Corean prince Amano Hiboko, settled at Hasama, province of Omi, where they manufactured a kind of pottery somewhat harder than that previously made.

After the successful invasion of Corea by the Japanese Empress Jingô, in A.D. 200, several Coreans settled in Japan, and made pottery.

In 463 some Japanese princes introduced from Petsi a number of colonists, among whom were some potters; but these were stated to have belonged to a Chinese corporation established in Corea.

Coreans were likewise concerned in establishing the factory at Karatsu (Hizen) at the end of the seventh century, the Raku fabric at Kiôto about 1550, another at Seto about 1590, and somewhat later one at Hagi. The principal fabric however which they had to do with is the well-known one of Satsuma, where the kilns were built on Corean models, and the potters formed a class apart, not being allowed to marry out of their own community.*

* Mr. Ernest Satow has published in the "Transactions of the Asiatic Society of Japan " [1878] an interesting account of his visit to these potteries.

Excepting, however, the Satsuma ware, the Coreans do not appear to have introduced any pottery of remarkable excellence, and we hear nothing of their porcelain-making. We have already explained one of the reasons for this constant introduction of Corean potters; any merits in Japanese pottery must have originated with the Japanese themselves, or have been derived from China.

The Chinese influence produced more important results. In 1223 Kato Shirozayemon, better known as Tôshiro, returned from China, where he had been to study the art of making pottery. He settled at Seto (Owari), and made a glazed stoneware, employing for the earlier specimens Chinese clay.

For the manufacture of porcelain the Japanese are also indebted to the Chinese, though this was not introduced till the sixteenth century. In 1513 Gorodayu Shonsui of Isé returned from China and settled in the province of Hizen. The porcelain which he made was chiefly on the Chinese models, and only ornamented with blue painting. The various porcelain factories of Hizen seem to have been established on the principle introduced by him.

In 1799 there were no less than eighteen factories in the neighbourhood of Imari in that province.* Two of them, Okawaji and Mikawaji, did not make their wares for sale, being the private factories of the princes of Saga and Hirato respectively. Of the factories producing porcelain for sale, it is stated that only one decorated its wares with colours and gilding, and from it must have proceeded the great quantity of porcelain known to us under the name of "Old Japan." This, as will appear from the Report, was first made in 1641 for exportation to China, probably to supply the Portuguese market at Macao, and afterwards exported by the Dutch to all parts of Europe. It would be very interesting to know whence was derived the peculiar style of decoration, which

* See Dr. Hoffmann's translation from a Japanese work in Stanislas Julien, Hist. de la Porcelaine chinoise, Paris, 1856.

is evidently not borrowed from the Chinese. The sets of vases would be useless in a Japanese house, there being no place on which they could be stood ; and their rarity in that country is shown by their being seldom now received, and by the high prices which are asked for them ; for instance, the large vase No. 169, though the cover has been completed in metal, was priced at £80 13s. The factories of Hizen have not lost their old reputation, and in the Paris Exhibition of 1878 numerous specimens, remarkable for size and decoration, were exhibited.

We have spoken of the pottery of Seto, but its porcelain has considerable merit, and, though the factory is of more recent origin than those of Hizen, it has oddly enough given its name to porcelain, which is often known in Japan as *Setomono* or Seto ware.

The Kutani factory was founded in the seventeenth century by Tamura Gonzayemon, and was improved by Gotô Saijiro, who had studied porcelain-making in Hizen. Its earlier productions are a coarse kind of porcelain, decorated in strong colours; but, later, this gave way to the well-known red decoration, familiar to us under the name of Kaga, chiefly used on a fine yellow pottery.

The Satsuma ware, so much esteemed by European collectors, was made at first in small quantities for the use of the Prince of Satsuma and his friends. The decoration in colours was not introduced till the end of the last century. Most of the specimens sold as old Satsuma have been made at Ôta and Awata in recent times.

The various wares made at Kiôto, by Ninsei and his followers, Kenzan, and others, are noticed in the Report. All these Kiôto fabrics are remarkable for their quaint and fanciful forms, owing, no doubt, to their being made at the city in which the Mikado resided, and for the use of his courtiers.

Of the history of the other factories it is scarcely necessary to speak, being of less importance than those we have mentioned, and sufficiently described in the Report.

The Ceramic wares of Japan exhibit great differences in their composition, texture, and appearance, but may be roughly classed under three principal heads: 1. Common pottery and stoneware, generally ornamented simply by scoring and glazing the surface. 2. A cream-coloured faïence, with a glaze, often crackled, and delicately painted in colours. 3. Hard porcelain.

To the first of these classes belong the wares of Bizen, old Seto, Shigaraki, and other small fabrics, including the Raku wares.

The principal factories of the second class are Awata, Satsuma, and the recent imitations of the latter at Ôta and elsewhere.

Among the porcelain the coarsest is that made at Kutani, but the most celebrated fabrics are in the province of Hizen, at Seto in Owari, and Kiyomidzu near Kiôto.

The substances used by the Japanese in making their wares are very numerous and varied, and to describe them fully here would take more space than is desirable. Some account of them may be found at the end of M. Julien's translation of the " History of the Porcelain of King-te-chin," communicated by Dr. Hoffmann, but they are treated of more fully in the second part of " Le Japon à l'Exposition universelle de 1878," published under the authority of the Japanese Commission.

It may be sufficient to remark that the porcelain of Japan is made in a different way from that of China. Having been fashioned, it is baked in a biscuit state, then painted with such colours as require a great heat, and the glaze applied ; then burnt again at a much higher temperature ; any further decoration in enamel colours, or gilding, being subsequently fired in a muffle kiln. These numerous firings show that the clays used in Japan are less tenacious than those used in China, hence Japanese specimens are frequently slightly out of shape, and they seem to require numerous supports in the kiln, which have left those scars on the glaze known as "spur marks." Saggars are said to have been first introduced into the manufactory at Arita in 1770, and are only employed for the choicer specimens.

The Japanese have applied cloisonné enamel and lacquer to some of their wares, and, indeed, seem to have sought for every possible variety of effect, so as to render any classification of their products a matter of great difficulty. This is no doubt partly due to the individual character of Japanese art, much of the pottery being produced in very small kilns, worked by a single family.

### Shapes and Uses of Vases.

We have already mentioned the vases used in the tea ceremony : the furnace, water vessel, jar to hold the powdered tea, pan for ashes, and tea bowl. The furnace (*furo*) varied somewhat in form ; it generally consisted of a globular vessel on three legs, and with openings in the upper part to create a draught ; into this upper part fitted the vessel in which the water was boiled, a smaller repetition of the same form, with two handles and a lid. The water vase (*midzu-sashi*) to hold a supply of water for washing the utensils, was generally rudely made, and often with a lacquer cover (Nos. 49, 65, etc.). The tea jar (*cha-ire*), of which numerous specimens exist in this collection, is generally a small oviform vase of hard pottery, with no decoration beyond its mottled glaze, and with a flat lid of ivory. This is often encased in a rich silk bag, which again is occasionally enclosed in a lacquer box, with an outer bag of a coarser material. They are all of small size, as the green tea which they contained was powdered and very strong, besides being very costly. The tea bowl (*cha-wan*) is purposely very rudely made, and of somewhat varied shapes, some being very shallow bowls, resembling saucers, others nearly cylindrical. As the tea was not only made in the bowl but drunk out of it, great care was taken that the edges should be smooth to the lips. The decoration, as will be seen, is so very slight as to scarcely deserve the name. The ash pan (*hai-ki*) is a shallow pan of unglazed ware, with edge curved inwards.

We next come to vessels employed in incense burning, which, as we have seen, forms part of the tea ceremony, but was likewise a favourite pastime among the Japanese nobles of old times. The game consisted in guessing the name of the perfume which was being burnt, with the usual forfeits, etc. We find here incense boxes (*kogo*) of the most varied forms, generally small in size. The incense burner (*koro*) varies also considerably, sometimes taking the forms of men, animals, or birds. The lower part of the · vessel was filled with a fine white ash, on which a piece of lighted charcoal was placed, and again upon this the incense. This arrangement will account for few of the incense burners showing any marks of fire on the lower part, though plentiful traces of smoke may be observed on their lids and elsewhere.

The only vessel connected with tobacco smoking which is made in pottery is the fire-holder, from which the smoker lights his pipe. This vessel is generally of small size, and cylindrical in form, to fit into the lacquer smoking-box in which the Japanese keep all their apparatus for smoking.

For keeping the hands warm a small earthenware brazier (*shiu-ro*) was used, somewhat pear-shaped in form, with an opening on one side. This vessel is sometimes very quaintly shaped; for instance, No. 115, in the form of an extremely fat woman. Another shape will be found under No. 107.

The objects for use at the writing-table consist of small ornamental screens, used also as paper weights, vases for washing the brushes or pencils used in writing, vases for holding them, and small closed vessels for supplying water to the inkstand. These last are very various in form, but all have a diminutive spout to allow the water to issue drop by drop, and a small hole on which to place the finger to regulate the flow.

The vases for saké drinking are chiefly bottles, either square, round, or polygonal, and jugs with spouts something like kettles or tea pots.   The saké is generally drunk out of small porcelain cups, sometimes graduated in size.

The tea pots (*dobin*) are generally of two forms—one like the ordinary European vessel, the other (*kiu-su*) with a hollow handle at right angles to the spout.   This latter was first introduced in the fifteenth century.

The cups are of the ordinary form, but without handles; a saucer, when there is one, serves only as a stand for the cup.   At their meals plates and dishes are used, but chiefly of a saucer shape, the flat edge being made only to suit European habits.   Small bowls are used for eating rice, an invariable feature of a Japanese meal, but the rice is served in a large wooden or lacquer bowl. Boxes to contain cakes may be found in the collection, of varied and elegant forms.   Small saucers are used to hold comfits. Coarse pottery is naturally employed for all kinds of kitchen uses, gardening and agriculture, among others for steeping rice and other grains (No. 43).

In ornamental pieces we find a number of figures, both of men and animals.   The flower vases form a large class.   As in China so in Japan, the people have a great admiration for flowers, and it is considered that every season or festival is to be marked by the presence of its appropriate floral decoration.   Their nosegays, however, are very different from ours—a picturesque disposition of a piece of old fir-tree and one or two other plants being the end to be attained.   It is scarcely necessary to describe the ordinary flower vases (*hana-ike*); but one class, the hanging flower vases attached to the beam of the room, deserve notice from their quaint and fantastic character.   The most varied forms are sought for— a bunch of wisteria (*fuji*), an old pine cone, a section of bamboo, a gourd, a firefly, a swallow beating as it were against the wall, are designs that may be found in these vases.   It is a question whether what we are pleased to call decorative vases belong to the proper native Japanese taste; they are either copies of Chinese originals or made for the European market.   Such objects would be quite out of place in a Japanese interior. Moreover, pairs of vases would be quite contrary to Japanese fancy, which abhors symmetry.

## DECORATION.

To make clear the motives of decorative ornament among the Japanese it is necessary to give some idea of the principles which guide them, and the influences by which they are governed.

There are two principal religions in Japan, the old national religion, the Kami worship, and Buddhism—the latter subdivided into numerous sects. Of the former we rarely find any representations on the Ceramic wares, nor, excepting in figures, do we often find any of Buddha or his followers. There are, however, seven divinities in Japan who have been partially adopted by the Buddhists, and who seem to constitute the real popular mythology of that country, and these or their symbols are frequently depicted on pottery. These are the seven gods of Good Fortune, of which the names are as follows :

1. Fukurokujiu, the god of Longevity, distinguished by an abnormal development of head, a long beard, and carrying a rough staff; his chief attributes are a sacred tortoise and a stork, and he is sometimes attended by a white stag. (See Fig. 6, p. 33.)

2. Yebis, brother of the Sun, the god of Daily Bread, represented as a fisherman, occasionally with a large fish attached to his rod, fish being a favourite food of the Japanese.

3. Daikoku, the god of Riches, a short figure, holding a miner's hammer, and seated on or near bales of rice ; he often has a large bag, and, quaintly enough, is not unfrequently attended by rats, though they are more likely to impoverish than enrich the owners of the rice. His attributes are emblems of the great sources of wealth in Japan, rice cultivation and mines. In former times the wealth of the Daimios was calculated by the number of *kokus* of rice their estates produced, and the quantity of copper and gold obtained from their mines.

4. Hotei, the god of Contentment, a fat old man with a bare

belly, holding a bag and a hand screen. He is often accompanied by children, who play all kinds of tricks with this good-natured Diogenes of Japan.

5. Jurojin, a dignified figure, in the costume of a learned man, carrying rolls of writing on the end of a staff, and holding a hand-screen ; a young stag follows his footsteps.

6. Bishamon, the god of Military Glory, dressed as a warrior, and holding a spear and a small pagoda.

7. Benten, the goddess of Love, richly dressed ; sometimes attended by fifteen boys, her children.

Of these divinities the first four are the most popular, and few Japanese households are without figures of some of them on their domestic altars.   Notwithstanding this universal *cultus* their devotees are apt to treat them with great familiarity in their representations, often depicting them in ridiculous attitudes and costumes. Most of them may generally be recognised as supernatural beings by a great development of the lobes of the ears.

Historical subjects but rarely occur, and only on specimens of comparatively modern origin.   Scenes from domestic life are more common.   In landscapes the Peerless Mountain, Fujiyama, may frequently be seen, with its remarkable snow-capped cone. The beautiful lake and river scenery of Japan furnish the materials for most of the landscape decoration, though, as a rule, preference is given to designs of a simpler character.

In drawing quadrupeds it cannot be said that the Japanese show a marked success.   The principal of those represented are the horse, buffalo, deer, tiger, and dogs.   We occasionally also find the two animals about which the Japanese have invented a number of superstitious stories, the badger* (*tanuki*) and the fox (*kitsuné*), whose transformations are the subjects of many a tale. In their representation of birds the Japanese are pre-eminent : the crane as the emblem of longevity is most commonly represented, sometimes in flocks flying across the sun.  We also find eagles and

---

* This is really the Racoon-faced dog (*Nyctcreutes procyonoides*).

hawks, pheasants, ducks, domestic fowls, and small birds of various kinds.

The fishes are also excellent in drawing, and we may especially notice the *tai* fish, somewhat like our bream, the great object of predilection of Japanese gourmets, and the *koi*, a sort of carp, usually represented leaping up a cascade. Insects occur, but not in great abundance, and are well pictured. Before leaving the animals it should be mentioned that the Japanese zodiac consists entirely of animal forms, and that the set is often to be found in porcelain figures.

Of monstrous animals there are five which are very commonly depicted. 1. The dragon (*riô*), borrowed no doubt from the Chinese, which may be seen among clouds, or rising from the stormy waves of the ocean ; it has not, however, the same imperial signification that it bears in China. 2. The phœnix (*hoho*), which to a certain extent occupies the place of the Chinese dragon, being the emblem of imperial dignity in Japan. This fabulous bird is frequently seen in combination with other imperial emblems, to which we shall have occasion to refer hereafter. 3. The kirin, the kylin of the Chinese, a monstrous animal with the body and hoofs of a deer, the tail of a bull, and with a horn on its forehead. 4. A lion monster also occurs, again derived apparently from the Chinese, and remarkable from the numerous tufts of curly hair issuing from its body. A good example of this animal in Bizen ware may be seen under No. 34. 5. The sacred tortoise (*kamé*), an emblem of longevity, and found associated with the bamboo, fir, and other objects symbolising long life. With the exception of a broad hairy tail, it resembles the ordinary tortoise.

The Japanese are evidently close students of nature in their representation of trees and plants. Of the trees there are three which commonly occur in combination, and which are special favourites. These are the fir, the bamboo, and the plum, which are collectively known by a modification of their Chinese names as *sho chiku bai*, and form an emblem of longevity.

c

Anyone familiar with Japanese porcelain will have noticed the exquisite delicacy with which the grasses and other flowers of the garden or the field are rendered. The nelumbium, or sacred water-lily, as an emblem of Buddha, frequently occurs; the chrysanthemum, furnishing what may be called the imperial arms of Japan; the iris; the peony, of which innumerable varieties are cultivated. Gourds also appear, being connected to a certain extent with longevity.

In simple ornaments, we should call attention to the fondness of the Japanese for disposing their designs in panels of strange and irregular shape, often represented overlapping each other, and

Kiku-mon,
Imperial Badge of Japan.

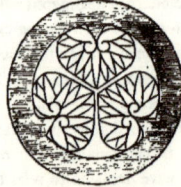

Badge of the
Tokugawa Family.

without any regard to symmetry. Any spare spaces, borders, etc., are filled with diapers, of which the variety is endless, all possessing quaintness and many of them great beauty. Among these are to be found the Greek fret and other patterns, which we are apt to associate with classic times.

Among these ornaments we occasionally find in a conspicuous position some of the badges that constitute Japanese heraldry. The chrysanthemum, or *kiku-mon*, is the badge of the Empire of Japan (see woodcut). It is treated in a very conventional manner, by no means resembling the natural flower. The family of the Mikado (the most ancient reigning family in the world) has, as a badge, three leaves and flowers of the *Paulownia imperialis*, known as the *kiri-mon*, also treated conventionally. (See woodcut.) The later Shoguns belonged to the Tokugawa family, and therefore bore their own arms, three mallow leaves within a circle, their points meeting in the centre. The Prince of Soma had as his cognisance a prancing horse, tethered, in allusion to his name (*ma* = horse) (see p. 103), as well as eight balls surrounding a larger central one. All the other nobles had cognisances of a like character with which they distinguished their furniture and accoutrements ; but they occur less often on pottery and porcelain, though in some cases they may have suggested the motif of the ornament.

Kiri-mon,
The Badge of the Mikado's Family.

MARKS.

On Chinese porcelain the marks chiefly consist of a date, the names of the halls at which it was made, inscriptions commending the specimens, or ornamental devices, none of which throw any light on the exact locality of the manufacture.

The Japanese marks are far more instructive. Dates indeed are less frequent than with the Chinese, but we occasionally find the Japanese *nengo*, which like the Chinese *nien-hao*, is an arbitrary name given to the reign, or a portion of the reign, of an emperor.*

* Lists of these Japanese *nengos* may be found in Siebold's " Nipon," Jacquemart et Le Blant, "Histoire de la Porcelaine," Hooper and Phillips, " Manual of Marks," and in the list printed by Mr. E. Satow.

C 2

We frequently find the names of places at which the wares were made, or sometimes the names by which they are known, for instance, Asahi, Minato, etc.

The most common mark, however, on Japanese wares, is the name of the potter (in this particular very unlike the Chinese), owing, no doubt, to the individual character given by the Japanese workman to his productions, and to the small size of the factory at which they were made. In China every piece passes through the hands of a number of workmen, each contributing his fraction to the decoration. All these decorators being other than the potter who turned the vase, and the workman who glazed it, no single specimen could be marked as the work of one man. In Japan it is far otherwise; the factory is small, carried on by a single potter and his own family, and he naturally therefore was proud to add his name as a guarantee of its origin. This is more particularly the case in the older wares, made chiefly for home consumption. The rich porcelain exported to Europe had inscribed on it a false Chinese date, or a device of no meaning. Ornaments were rarely used as marks, except where it was intended to imitate Chinese porcelain.

The Japanese make use of three modes of writing, all derived to a certain extent from the Chinese. They use the true Chinese character either in the *chuan* or seal form, or in the *kien shu* or common character, and these are most frequently to be met with as marks; but we also find the *kata kana*, a syllabic writing of forty-eight characters, invented by the Japanese from portions of Chinese words, and likewise the *hira kana*, an abbreviated and running form, also modified from the Chinese, the characters being also forty-eight in number.

The mark is sometimes scratched, sometimes impressed with a seal, sometimes painted. It will be noticed in the Report that occasionally some of the princes bestowed on potters of note seals to be used on their wares.

It is much to be regretted that the Japanese have been so much in the habit of inscribing on their productions the Chinese dates, which has been done without the slightest regard to the age of the specimens. The Chinese dates *Seuen tih* and *Ching hwa* are both to be found on Japanese porcelain, though both of them had passed away before the art of making porcelain had been introduced into Japan. It was these dates which led M. Jacquemart into the error of attributing to the Chinese the large class of porcelain which he has termed "chrysanthémo-pæonienne," and which he should at a glance have seen to be totally different from the productions of the Celestial Empire.

JAPANESE CRANE,
an Emblem of Longevity.

# JAPANESE REPORT

AND

## CATALOGUE OF THE SPECIMENS.

---

### ANCIENT WARES.

OLD Japanese Legends attribute the invention of pottery to Oosui-tsumi, who lived in the time of Oanamuchi-no-mikoto, long before the historical period of Japan, which dates from B.C. 660.

Mr. Ninagawa, archæologist in the Imperial Museum at Tokio, writes: "We testify that pottery was made in times most remote, from the fact that it is stated in the earliest Japanese history, entitled 'Nihongi,' that Sosanowo-no-mikoto, brother of Amaterasu-oho-mi-kami, advised Tenatsuchi to prepare from different fruits a drink, in eight 'vases.'" He adds: "We are unacquainted with any specimens of these ancient productions." This Sosanowo-no-mikoto was contemporary with Oosui-tsumi. The Emperor Jimmu, in the first year of his reign (B.C. 660), instructed an official of the name of Wakanetsu-hiko-no-mikoto to manufacture various kinds of pottery to be used in the temple for religious services. He succeeded in producing a coarse kind of earthenware from a clay found at Amanokaku-yama, in the province of Yamato. This ware, which derives its name from its shape, is known as *Hiraka* and *Itsuka*. At this time pottery was

probably fashioned by hand. It was placed in a pit in the
ground and covered with timber which was then fired. When
the heat had reached a certain intensity the timber was removed
and the contents covered with dry earth and left to cool.

In consequence of the impossibility of obtaining an equal
temperature throughout the kiln, there being no draught, articles

Fig. 1. Ancient Vase, *circa* B.C. 640. No. 1.

from the same baking are often of different colours. There is in
this collection a specimen which appears to have been made by
this process. (No. 1.) Even at the present day the vessels used
in the temples of the villages of Hatayenoki-no-mura, in the
province of Yamashiro, and Kasuga, in the province of Yamato,
are fashioned by hand and baked in small kilns.

In the early part of the reign of the Emperor Suinin (B.C. 27) the

Corean prince, Hiboko, settled at Hasama, in the province of Omi, where his followers manufactured a kind of ware somewhat harder than the preceding, and marked on the exterior with small lines.

After the Corean invasion by the Empress Jingô Kogo (A.D. 200) several Corean potters settled in Japan, since which time the manufacture has progressed rapidly. Ware of this period is marked on the bottom with a figure resembling waves. In the time of the Emperor Yuriaku in A.D. 473, an official named Haji-no-muraji was commanded to provide pottery for use at the dining-table. In evidence of the art having developed and spread throughout the country, it is recorded that the Emperor received offers for the supply of such vessels from many different places : Kusasa-mura, in the province of Settsu ; Uji-mura and Fushimi-mura, in the province of Yamashiro ; Fujikata-mura, in the province of Isé ; and from manufactories in the provinces of Tamba, Tajima, etc.

Many of these places still preserve their old tradition.

A kind of unglazed earthenware is made by the people of Kusasa-mura ; and the ancient art is carried on at Uji, where Asahi-yaki is made (No. 54), Fushimi (No. 100), Fuka-kusa, and neighbourhood, and also in the provinces of Tamba and Inaba. At Fujikata-mura pieces of this ancient pottery are occasionally dug up, confirming the locality of the factory.

In the first year of the Emperor Mommu (A.D. 696), a special officer was appointed to supervise and encourage the trade of pottery-making, and a priest named Giyogi, a native of the province of Idzumi, invented the potter's wheel, and instructed the people in the method of using it. Samples of earthenware actually made by him are to be seen in the temple of Todaiji, in the province of Yamato.

The Giyogi yaki, as this ware is generally termed, is of a glossy dark colour, and of great solidity. (No. 2.) An older ware is occasionally dug up in the same locality, and has sometimes been mistaken for it.

1. VASE (*magatama tsubo*); rough pale-red ware, with irregular patches of black and grey; round the upper part of the body is a convoluted pattern slightly in relief, with indented diagonal lines. Silk cover. Said to have been used at religious festivals about 640 B.C. H. 6⅞ in. diam. 6⅞ in. [Figure 1.]      160.77.

Fig. 2. Flask, *circa* A.D. 730. No. 2.

2. FLASK-SHAPED BOTTLE; grey ware, showing on one face the marks of the wheel; slightly expanding mouth, and two hooks as handles on the shoulders. It is enclosed in a slight framework of rattan. Used at religious festivals. Said to be made by Giyogi, about A.D. 730. H. 8¾ in. diam. 7⅞ in. [Figure 2.]      161.77.

### KARATSU WARE.

The manufactory is situated at the foot of a hill near the harbour of Karatsu, in the province of Hizen, and seems to have been founded towards the end of the seventh century. It may be considered as the earliest glazed pottery made in Japan; the name of the founder, however, is unknown. The first productions were a kind of faïence, but stoneware was also made; both these wares are of great rarity. They are classified according to the periods of their manufacture. 1st. From the foundation of the pottery to the period Kenchô (A.D. 1249–55). 2nd. From the period Kenchô to the period Yeiroku (1558–69). 3rd. From the period Yeiroku to the beginning of the period Keichô (1596), and are commonly called *Ko-Karatsu*, which means "old Karatsu," or *Yoné-hakari*, designating "rice measure," a name applied to a large bowl for measuring rice, beans, etc., in use before the exact measure of capacity had been fixed by the Emperor Mommu in A.D. 702. The 1st class is composed exclusively of white clay, whereas the 2nd class is of white or red clay.

The factory was probably erected by Coreans, who frequently came to Japan about this period, and the ware produced much resembles that of Corean manufacture. (No. 3.) In the time of Kôji and Yeiroku (1555–69) the tea ceremony had become in favour, and had increased the demand for Corean pottery, which was then very rare. This caused the Karatsu manufacturer to make an imitation of the Corean work, which is now called *Oku-korai* (No. 4), meaning "old Corean," in order to distinguish it from the true Corean manufacture. A special variety, called *Ye-Karatsu* (painted Karatsu), was made in A.D. 1590. The designs, resembling the Corean, but not glossy, were under the glaze. In the oldest specimens they are not sufficiently clear to be made out. Ware made between the years A.D. 1600–54 is known as *Chiu-ko-Karatsu*, or "middle old Karatsu" (Nos. 6 and 7), while the later ware is generally called Karatsu yaki (No. 8).

Whilst the manufactory of Chiu-ko-karatsu was in operation, a clay was imported from Corea for the purpose of making tea utensils, for the use of those with whom the tea ceremony had become a favourite custom. Pottery made of this clay is very light and is called *Chosen Karatsu* (Corean Karatsu). From A.D. 1690 to 1730 the number of factories had very much increased, and many skilful potters had arisen, most prominent among them being Taroyemon, Yojibei, and Kiheiji (son of Taroyemon). The trade was almost entirely confined to the manufacture of tea utensils, and little attention was paid to the encouragement of art, in consequence of which it has much declined. There are at present no good workmen, and the manufacture has been to a great extent suspended.

Sixty or seventy years since, some people, in endeavouring to bring the art to greater perfection, succeeded in making, of Corean clay, a ware similar to the specimen No. 9 in this collection. In the Middle Ages a Chinaman of the name of Abo manufactured ware coated with a bluish glaze, called from him " Abo glaze."

3. TEA BOWL (*cha-wan*); red ware, covered inside, and partly outside, with a thickish grey glaze, somewhat granular in texture. Reproduction of the ancient Ko-Karatsu ware, of 1000 years ago. Made at Karatsu, about A.D. 1700. H. 3 in. diam. 4⅞ in.
162.77.

4. TEA BOWL (*cha-wan*); reddish-brown ware, covered with a drab glaze, blistered on the outside. Imitation of old Corean ware, called Oku-korai, made at Karatsu about 1550 H. 3¼ in. diam. 5½ in. 163.77.

5. TEA BOWL (*cha-wan*), slightly diminishing at the mouth, which has a small rim; reddish-brown ware, covered inside, and partly outside, with a pinkish-drab glaze, minutely crackled; round the upper part are rudely painted three scrolls in greyish-black. Ye-Karatsu ware, made at Karatsu, about A.D. 1590. diam. 4¾ in. 164.77.

6. TEA BOWL (*cha-wan*); coffee-coloured ware, covered with a thin sugary-drab glaze; on one side is a repair fixed with lacquer. Chiu-ko-Karatsu ware, made at Karatsu, about A.D. 1650. H 3 in. diam. 4½ in. 165.77.

7. SHALLOW TEA JAR (*cha-ire*) with hinged lid of ivory and wood;
brown ware, covered inside, and partly out, with a deep yellowish-
brown glaze. Chiu-ko-Karatsu ware, made at Karatsu, about
A.D. 1650. H. 1¼ in., diam. 3⅞ in.                166.77.

8. TALL CYLINDRICAL TEA BOWL (*naga cha-wan*); brown ware,
covered with a stone-coloured glaze, on which are rudely painted
flowers in brown. Karatsu ware, made at Karatsu,
about A.D. 1720. H. 3¼ in., diam. 3 in.  167.77.

9. WATER JAR (*midzu-ire*) of depressed globular
form; of pale reddish-brown stoneware; entirely
covered, in the first instance, with a pale brown
glaze, then mottled with a deep brown with slight
touches of sage green. Round the body are
incised scrolls and circles, round the mouth a
Greek fret, and round the base a Vandyke pattern.
All these ornaments are filled in with white paste,
under a transparent glaze; on the bottom a spiral
in relief and a mark scratched, *Shichi-jū ni sai
Ni-raku saku*, "Made by Niraku at the age of
seventy-two." Karatsu ware, made at Karatsu, about A.D. 1800.
H. 5⅜ in. diam. 8 in.                168.77.

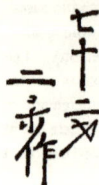

Fig. 3. Karatsu.
No. 9.

### SETO WARE.

This ware is manufactured at a village called Seto, in the
province of Owari. Its origin is of great antiquity, and cannot
now be ascertained. It is, however, stated in the Yengi-shiki (a
ceremonial record of the period Yengi, compiled in A.D. 927)
that a kind of pottery had been submitted to the Emperor, but
there are no known examples. Great progress was made by
Kato-Shirozayemon,* who went to China, in A.D. 1223, for five
years, with a priest named Dogen, for the purpose of studying
the art of pottery-making. Soon after his return he started a
manufactory in the province of Bizen, but his efforts were unsuc-
cessful. He then attempted the manufacture of porcelain at
various places in the province of Yamashiro and also in a
neighbouring district, but without any better success. The next

* [Ninagawa gives the name as Kato-Shiroyemon.]

scene of his enterprise was Kiôto (old capital) and its environs, and as far as the provinces of Owari and Mino. Eventually he discovered a good clay at a place called Oba-ga-futokoro, in the village of Seto. Here he set up a kiln called Heishi-kama and again commenced work. Ware made with clay brought from China is called by the tea-drinkers Kara-mono, meaning "Chinese ware," while that made from Seto clay is known as Ko-Seto.

Previously to his visit to China Kato-Shirozayemon had been engaged at Agatsu-mura in making a pottery known as *Horidashité*,* which had been very much admired by the tea-drinkers. This ware was much inferior to that which he afterwards produced.

His finest and most valuable work was in tea utensils, as, for instance, his tea jars and tea bowls, which, however, were not real porcelain, but of a kind of stoneware distinguished in Japan by the name of *Ishi-yaki.*

He had probably not become well initiated in the art in China, for the most prominent Chinese factories were in their decline, and his time for studying was limited. Although his productions were not of such fine porcelain as that made in China, yet they were received with great favour, inasmuch as one small tea bowl cost some thousand dollars in the time of Taiko Hideyoshi, when the tea ceremony had become more fashionable; and even now his work is considered as *Dai-mei-Butsu*, meaning "most valuable thing."

His name, Kato-Shirozayemon, has been abbreviated to Tôshiro, his other name being Shiun-kei. The ware made by him is called *Ko-Seto.* His descendants until the fourth generation assumed the same name, and their work is distinguished by prefixing the number of the generation. The ware made by the second Tôshiro is called simply by his name, and is not equal to that of the third Tôshiro.†

* [*Horidashité* really signifies the castaways found on the sites of ancient kilns.]

† [This third Tôshiro is called by Ninagawa Tôjiro, and his work is known under the name of *Mannaka-Kobutsu.* The fourth was called Tosaburo.]

In A.D. 1801 Kato Tamikichi, a potter, brother of Kato-Kichizayemon, went to Arita, in the province of Hizen, where he married the daughter of a porcelain manufacturer established there.

He remained for four years for the purpose of studying porcelain-making, and then returned to the province of Owari, where he succeeded in making, with a clay he had found, porcelain decorated with blue painting under the glaze, and

Fig. 4. Tea Jar, Seto ware. No. 11.

known as *sometsuké.* Since this time the trade has continued to increase.

The prominent makers of the present day are Kawamoto Hansuké, Kawamoto Masukichi, etc. etc. The latter is especially skilful in making large plates or tables of *sometsuké,* some of which are from 5 ft. to 10 ft. in diameter. This manufactory has in fact the monopoly for works of this great size.

10. TEA JAR (*cha-tsubo*) of globular form, with short neck and four
loop handles on the shoulders ; brown stoneware, covered with
a brown glaze, with streaks of lighter and darker colours ; the

glaze extends inside the mouth and to within a short distance
of the foot. Ko-Seto ware, made at Seto, in imitation of the
work of the first Tôshiro by his second successor, about A.D.
1310. H. 10 in. diam. 8¾ in.  169.77.

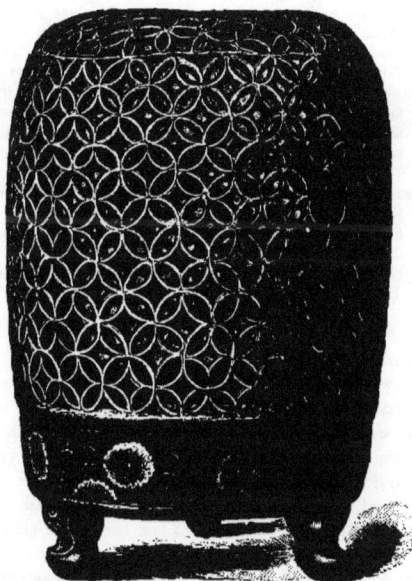

Fig. 5. Incense Burner, Seto ware. No. 13.

11. TEA JAR (*cha-ire*) of globular form, with ivory lid ; reddish-buff
stoneware, partially covered with a light and dark brown glaze.
On the bottom the concentric markings known by the Japanese
as *itoguiri*. Made at Seto about A.D. 1360. H. 2½ in.
[Figure 4.]  170.77.

12. SWORD RACK (*katana kake*) for two swords; porcelain, with
    ornaments in relief on a dark-blue ground, consisting of trunk
    and branches of the prunus. Made at Seto about A.D. 1820.
    H. 13½ in. I. 18½ in.                          171.77.
13. INCENSE BURNER (*koro*) in the form of a cylindrical cage of
    interlacing circles, resting on a stand with three small feet.
    White porcelain, with scrolls on the stand painted in blue.
    Made at Seto about A.D. 1830.  H. 7½ in. diam. 4⅞ in.
    [Figure 5.]                                    172.77.
14. TABLE of European form; circular top, baluster stem, with tripod
    foot; porcelain, painted in blue; on the top fishes among
    waves; on the stem and foot are scattered circles containing
    waves, heraldic badges, etc.  Made at Seto, by Kawamoto
    Masukichi, A.D. 1875.  H. 28½ in. diam. 30 in.      173.77.
15. PAIR OF FLOWER VASES (*hana-ike*), cylindrical bodies, rounded
    shoulders, short neck, and two handles; porcelain, covered with
    a brilliant coffee-coloured glaze, with ornaments left white; on
    the body of each two sprigs of large flowers; on the shoulders,
    clouds, etc.  Made at Seto by Kawamoto Masukichi, A.D. 1875.
    H. 17¼ in. diam. 6⅝ in.                         174.77.

## KI-SETO WARE.

This ware is also made in the province of Owari.  The
actory was founded in the periods Onin or Bunmei (1467–86)
by a man of the name of Haku-an.  Only six tea bowls made
by him are now known; they are in the possession of a Japanese
nobleman.  The name of the ware, *Ki-Seto*, meaning "yellow
Seto," is derived from the colour of the glaze.  The earliest works
are covered with a very fusible transparent glaze through which
the body can be seen.  Afterwards a thin but opaque glaze was
used, relieved by small transparent spots of a verdigris colour.
Representations of the plum flower, cherry-tree, chrysanthemum,
and creeping-grass, were also used in decorating it.  The
specimens of a deep yellow colour are considered the best, and
are very much appreciated by tea-drinkers.

16. SHALLOW TEA BOWL (*natsu cha-wan*, i.e. "summer tea bowl")
    of irregular form, being bent up at one side; brown ware,

covered with a pale yellowish-brown glaze, crackled. Ki-Seto ware, made in the province of Owari, about A.D. 1770, in imitation of an older ware of the 15th century. H. 3⅛ in. diam. 7½ in.  175.77.

17. FLOWER VASE (*hana-ike*), in the shape of a dice box; pale-buff stoneware, covered inside and out with a pale-yellow glaze; the bottom is rabbited at the edge, leaving in the centre a raised

Fig. 6. Fukurokujiu, Ki-Seto ware. No. 18.

circle with the *itoguiri* marks. Ki-Seto ware, made in the province of Owari, about A.D. 1670. H. 7⅝ in. diam. 5½ in.  176.77.

18. FIGURE of Fukurokujiu, the god of longevity, seated and opening a scroll; at his left side his attendant crane; yellow ware, covered with a thin glaze. Ki-Seto ware, made in the province of Owari, about A.D. 1800. H. 9⅜ in. [Figure 6.] 177.77.

D

## SHINO WARE.

This was another manufactory in the province of Owari. The produce was a kind of *ishi-yaki*, or stoneware, glazed with a very thick white enamel, crackled, and generally painted with gold powder. To the present day tea utensils and other articles are made there. The name is derived from Shino-soshin (of the fifteenth century), a great admirer of the ware. The best specimens are in the possession of a merchant in the city of Osaka.

19. TWO QUADRANGULAR FIRE POTS (*hi-ire*); pale ware, covered with a sugary light-grey glaze, crackled, and painted with rude floral ornaments in brown. Shino ware, made in the province of Owari, about A.D. 1570. H. 3⅚ in. 178.77.

## GEMPIN WARE.

This ware was made in the province of Owari by a Corean called Gempin,* who settled in the village of Seto about A.D. 1590. It is painted very roughly with cobalt under the glaze, which is of a whitish-grey colour.† (No. 20.)

The art perished with the founder, and specimens of the ware are of great rarity. There is preserved in Japan a pot (1 in. high, 3 in. diameter) used as an incense-burner: it is esteemed a rare and valuable object. It is of a kind of unglazed earthenware, and is engraved with one petal of the flower of *Nelumbo nucifera*; and both on the reverse and obverse are engraved lines of writing so exact and so fine as to be considered a masterpiece of penmanship.

20. CYLINDRICAL TEA BOWL (*cha-wan*); grey ware, with rudely painted ornament in pale bluish-green and covered with a grey glaze. Made at Seto about 1590 by a Corean named Gempin. H. 3¼ in. diam. 3¼ in. 179.77.

* [The Kojei Shiriyo says that he came to Japan as a refugee in 1659.]
† Cobalt painting had been practised years before, and was not a Corean invention.

## ORIBÉ WARE.

This ware was made at a factory in the province of Owari, founded in the beginning of the seventeenth century, in accordance with the request of a Hatamoto (subject of the Shogun or under his command), whose name was Furuta Oribé-no-sho Shigekatsu. The thickness of the second glaze was not uniform, and was often fused with an enamel of a verdigris colour. Some articles of this ware are decorated; others, though not the most valuable, are painted with a plum flower and latticed bars in dark brown, which design forms the coat-of-arms of the family of Furuta. At present, tea utensils and other inferior and smaller articles are made there.

21. TWO TRAYS (*sara*) of peculiar rectangular form, on three small feet; pale ware, covered with a thick sugary glaze of two colours, dark sage-green and salmon pink, divided by a cross line; the pink portion is ornamented with a whitish Vandyke pattern inside, and narrow vertical bands outside. Oribé ware, made in the province of Owari, about A.D. 1670. H. 1⅝ in. l. 4⅝ in. w. 4 in. 180.77.

## SETO-SUKÉ WARE.

This was first made by a native of the province of Owari, who studied the manufacture of porcelain at Seto, and who afterwards, in the periods Meiwa and Anyei (1764–80), set up a manufactory at Yokkaichi, in the province of Isé. True porcelain-making had already been practised, but there is no doubt that the art was developed and promoted by Tamikichi, who settled in the province of Hizen for the purpose of studying it, as aforesaid. (See *ante*, p. 30.)

瀬
戸
助

Fig. 7.
Seto-Suké.

22. TEA BOWL (*cha-wan*); coarse porcelain, painted in colours with a band of sixteen seated figures; the same repeated inside. Mark impressed, *Se-to-suké*, the name of the factory. [Figure 7.] Made at Yokkaichi, province of Isé, about A.D. 1780. H. 2⅝ in. diam. 4⅛ in. 181.77.

No. 22.

D 2

### SETO-KURO WARE.

This was made by Hirasawa Kuro, a native of Seto, in the province of Owari, who lived about the period Temmei (1781–88). He was very skilful in imitating different kinds of ancient pottery from every factory of Owari, and his work is so like that it is very difficult to distinguish it from the original.

23. CRESCENT-SHAPED FLOWER VASE for suspension (*funa-gata hana-ike*, i.e. "shape of a ship"); reddish-brown ware, partially covered with a mottled brown glaze. Seto-Kuro ware, made by Hirasawa Kuro, a native of Seto, about A.D. 1790. H. 5¾ in. l. 7¼ in.  182.77.

### INU-YAMA WARE.

This factory is situated in the village of Inakimura (near the castle of Inu-yama), in the county of Niwa, province of Owari, but the date of its foundation is unknown. It is, however, certain that in A.D. 1810 there was made here an imitation of Chinese porcelain (so-called Aka-yé), decorated with red ochre and also cobalt painting. The trade still flourishes.

24. FIVE-SIDED BOWL for cakes (*kwashi-bachi*); coarse porcelain, rudely painted with red flowers and green leaves; inside is the character, *kuwai*, "a chief;" below, on the bottom, the character *in*, "seal." Inu-yama ware, A.D. 1860. H. 2¾ in. diam. 5¾ in.  183.77.

### MINO WARE.

This ware is made at several villages in the province of Mino, the chief manufactory being at Tajimi-mura. The art was first introduced from the province of Owari into a village called Kushiri-mura, whence it spread to different parts of the province. During the seventeenth century the Emperor encouraged the factory with an order to make some pieces. The produce had been confined to a kind of earthenware until 1810, when the making of real porcelain was commenced. It is known as *Shin-sei*, designating "the new thing." There are still 110 kilns, where is produced porcelain decorated with cobalt under the glaze, which is somewhat more translucent than that made in the province of Owari.

Some of the ware is decorated with a design similar to that in vogue at Kiyomidzu in Kiôto, the western capital of Japan. (No. 25.)

25. PAIR OF FLOWER VASES (*hana-ike*); oviform bodies, and handles in the form of fishes; porcelain, covered with a reticulated pattern painted in blue. Mark, *Ni-pon Mi-no kuni Ka-to Go-suké sei*, " Made by Kato Gosuké, in the province of Mino, Japan." [Figure 8.] Made in 1875. H. 5¼ in.   184.77.

26. CYLINDRICAL CUP AND SAUCER; porcelain, painted with flowers in blue, delicately touched. Mark, same as the last. Made in 1875. H. of cup 3¼ in. diam. of saucer 5¼ in.   185.77.

日 加
本 籬
美 五
濃 輔
國 製

Fig.8. Mino. No. 25.

## BIZEN WARE.

Bizen ware is produced in the province of Bizen, and consists of three kinds, viz., *Bizen yaki, Imbe yaki,* and *Hita-suké.* The character of them is the same, but the appearance is different. The date of the commencement of the factory is not known; it is supposed that from the time of the Mikado Shujin (B.C. 97–30) there was very probably made there a kind of earthenware, for the ware now produced preserves the shapes of the vases used for religious festivals at a remote period. There is another proof in support of this theory, in the village where a factory existed being called in the old dialect Imbe-mura. Besides which, in the tenth year of the Mikado Shujin, there was made a vase called Imbe for temple use, which we may assume to have been made here.

A large kiln, founded in the year 1390, still exists in the village above-mentioned in the province of Aki, where six families are pursuing the trade. The ware made here has the same character as Bizen ware, but is a little smoother. (Nos. 41, 42.) On the hill of Kumayama, in the vicinity of Imbe-mura, are to be seen the ruins of an old kiln. The manufacture of stoneware, which is continued up to the present time, was commenced in 1210, and an inferior kind of ware was made for agricultural purposes, such as the vases used for keeping and germinating seeds, which are now called *Ko-Bizen,* meaning " old Bizen," in contradistinction to *Bizen Yaki,* or the later work, the manufacture of which was commenced in A.D. 1580. The production of small tea pots, flower vases, and vases for domestic use, dates from the period Tensho (A.D. 1573–91), and an inferior kind, chiefly for kitchen use, is still made. The work is composed of two kinds, viz. biscuit and thinly-glazed ware. The better kind is made of a white or light bluish clay, and well baked in order to receive the red-brown colour; whereas the commoner kind is of a red clay. They are very hard and solid, and well fitted to hold liquid. (Nos. 26–36.) There is another kind of ware known as *Migakité* (Nos. 37, 38) especially solid and glossy.

The Hitasuké, which is so called from its resembling a knotted or twisted cord, was first manufactured towards the close of the sixteenth century. It was made of very sandy clay, and is very porous. (Nos. 39, 40.)

27. TEA JAR (*cha-ire*); rough grey ware, reddened on one side; cylindrical in form, decreasing in size at the foot. The marks of the wheel form horizontal lines. Ivory lid and silk bag. Ko-Bizen ware, made in the province of Bizen, about 1370. H. 3¾ in. diam. 3½ in.        186.77.
28. DISH (*sara*), much misshapen, probably a castaway found on the site of a kiln ; coarse red ware, partly glazed ; around the inner edge a band of dull green. Ko-Bizen ware, made in the province of Bizen, about 1370. Diam. 11 in.        187.77.
29. CYLINDRICAL WATER JAR (*midzu-ire*); coarse red ware, discoloured in the firing ; round the outside edge is a broad irregular ridge; the lip is bent down inwards, and at the bottom is stamped twice a trifid object like a water-plantain leaf. Ko-Bizen ware, made about 1400. H. 6½ in. diam. 7 in.        188.77.

30. CYLINDRICAL TEA JAR (*cha-ire*); greenish-grey ware, with a patch of red on one side ; rudely made, and with vertical and horizontal lines incised on the sides. Ivory lid. Bizen ware, made about 1620. H. 2⅞ in. diam. 2⅜ in. 189.77.

31. INCENSE BURNER (*koro*) in the form of a figure of Hotei, the god of contentment, seated and laughing ; red ware, covered with a thin glaze. Bizen ware, made about 1680. H. 3¾ in.
190.77.

32. CYLINDRICAL WATER JAR (*midzu-ire*) with a handle on each side ; rudely shaped, and of red ware defectively glazed ; square seal stamped inside. Lacquer cover. Bizen ware, made about 1740. H. 8 in. 191.77.

33. ORNAMENT (*oki-mono*) in the form of Kinkosen (a Chinese saint) seated on a *koi* fish and holding a roll ; brown stoneware, slightly glazed. Bizen ware, made about 1770. H. 8 in. l. 11½ in. 192.77.

34. ORNAMENT (*oki-mono*) ; figure of a fantastic lion with large ears and tail ; red stoneware, slightly glazed. Bizen ware, made about 1770. H. 13 in. l. 2 ft. 7 in. 193.77.

35. INCENSE BURNER (*koro*), in the form of an ancient Chinese tripod cup (*tseo*) with an oval bowl pinched in at the sides, and three splay legs. Bizen ware, made about 1820. H. 3½ in. l. 4⅜ in. 194.77.

36. CAKE BOX (*ju-kumi*) in four stages, square in form ; bright chocolate ware, slightly glazed. It consists of four trays fitting one into the other, and has a cover with bevelled edges ; on the sides are incised branches of the pine, prunus, and bamboo, known to the Japanese in combination as *sho-chiku-bai* ; on the cover the sacred tortoise. On one side is inscribed *Ro-kei sei*, "Made by Rokei." [Figure 9.] Bizen ware, made about 1840. H. 8¾ in. w. 6⅝ in. 195.77.

芦
景
製

37. TEA BOWL (*cha-wan*) ; hard stoneware, covered with a thin mottled glaze, red and greenish-grey. Migakité ware, made in the province of Bizen, about 1670. H. 2¾ in. diam. 3½ in. 196.77.

Fig. 9. Bizen. No. 36.

38. WATER JAR (*midzu-ire*) of globular form, with ribbed shoulders and flat cover ; dark steel-grey stoneware ; round the lip studs in relief. Mark impressed on cover and bottom. [Figure 10.] Migakité ware, made in the province of Bizen, about 1760. H. 6⅝ in. diam. 7½ in. 197.77.

39. ASH BOWL (*hai-ki*), used at the tea ceremony; speckled drab ware, mottled with brick red. Mark stamped, two bars in a circle. [Figure 11.] Hitasuké ware, made in the province of Bizen, A.D. 1579. H. 2⅜ in. diam. 5¼ in.    198.77.

Fig. 10.  Fig. 11.
Bizen.  Bizen.
No. 38.  No. 39.

40. WATER JAR (*kata-kuchi*) with short spout on one side; grey ware, rudely made, and with horizontal furrows outside; it is ornamented with a few streaks of light red, irregularly disposed. Hitasuké ware, made in the province of Bizen, about 1850. H. 4½ in. diam. 7¾ in.    199.77.

41. TWELVE-SIDED TEA JAR (*cha-ire*); chocolate ware, glazed, and having on one side a patch of yellow. On the bottom the *itoguiri*. Ivory cover. Imbé ware, made in the province of Bizen, about 1640. H. 3⅝ in.    200.77.

42. FLOWER VASE (*hana-ike*), in the shape of a dice box; grey ware, horizontally ribbed, and covered with a thin greenish-grey glaze. Imbé ware, made in the province of Bizen, about 1720. H. 9 in.    201.77.

### SHIGARAKI WARE.

This ware is produced in a village named Nagano-mura, in Shigaraki, in the county of Koga, province of Omi. The origin of the factory is unknown, but it is supposed to have been founded about A.D. 1300. At first only inferior articles for domestic use were made. These are called *Ko-Shigaraki.* (Nos. 43, 44.) At the beginning of the sixteenth century, the ceremony having become more fashionable, the manufacture of tea utensils was introduced here as it had already been at other factories. About this time a renowned tea drinker of the name of Sho-o encouraged the manufacturer to make tea jars and flower vases solely for use at the tea ceremonies, and the ware then produced is called *Sho-o Shigaraki.* It is a description of *Ishi-yaki,* or stoneware, very hard and heavy, and glazed with an enamel of a deep yellowish-red, which is again covered in parts by pouring on to it an enamel, somewhat transparent, and of a verdigris colour. It is recorded that the tea-drinkers were much satisfied with the tasteful appearance of this ware, which closely resembled the productions of Corea, Annam, and one of the East India islands. There was a very thin and light quality of ware made here, but it is seldom to be met with. A ware manufactured between 1610 and 1650 is called *Sotan Shigaraki*, after one of the tea-drinkers. It is composed of white clay, and is very fairly glazed. The ceremony of tea-drinking steadily increased, and all the requisite utensils were made at the factory. Later a class of ware styled *Getaha* was produced ; on the bottom is impressed a mark resembling the impression of a Japanese clog.* In 1828 the Shogun of the Tokugawa family ordered the manufacture of a tea jar called Koshishiro-Tsukemimi; since then this factory has been noted for its tea jars, which are said to preserve successfully the flavour of the tea. In the vicinity there are eight villages, prominent among them being Kaméyama and Teshi, where oil cups for illuminating purposes, oil pitchers, tea jars, and the inferior flower vases used in the temples are made.

Afterwards, Hanzo, a native of Kinose-mura, made an inferior kind of porcelain for domestic use.

43. JAR (*tane-tsubo*) for steeping rice seed ; grey stoneware, covered with a thin brown glaze, with white specks. Ko-Shigaraki ware, made in the province of Omi, about 1420. H. 4¼ in.
202.77.

44. FIRE VASE for smokers (*hi-ire*) of a beehive shape, with small lid, and three holes pierced on the shoulder ; pale-red ware, with fragments of quartz dispersed through the paste. Ko-Shigaraki ware, made in the province of Omi, about 1420. H. 3½ in. diam. 4¾ in.
203.77.

45. TEA BOWL (*cha-wan*) ; pale ware, covered with a red glaze ; on one side a patch of greenish white. Shigaraki ware, made about 1660. H. 3½ in. diam. 4¼ in.
204.77.

---

* [This mark is called *Getaokoshi* by Ninagawa, and was produced by two wooden supports, on which the vase was placed before it was baked. The same process was used at Iga.]

## IGA WARE.

This factory, which is at Mambashira, province of Iga, adjoins that of Shigaraki in the province of Omi, and appears to have been founded about the same time. There is a ware called *Ko-Iga*, which is closely allied to Shigaraki ware, but being baked harder it is rathèr darker. Small articles only are now made.

46. FLOWER VASE (*hana-ike*), very rudely made, and with two projecting ears as handles ; pale grey stoneware, covered with a greenish glaze, and with irregular patches of brown. On the body a stamp three times repeated, being an oblong with two rows of squares, in each of which is a dot. Iga ware, made in the province of Omi, about 1650. H. 10½ in. diam. 5⅞ in.

205.77.

47. TEA JAR (*cha-ire*), barrel shaped ; pale-red ware, the upper part and inside covered with a brown glaze, mottled with green, etc. Ivory cover. Iga ware, made in the province of Omi, about 1650. H. 3⅞ in. diam. 2¼ in. 206.77.

48. SQUARE INCENSE BOX (*ko-go*) ; very coarse grey ware, rudely made, covered with a transparent glaze. Iga ware, made in the province of Omi, about 1650. W. 1⅞ by 1¼ in. 207.77.

## TAMBA WARE.

A kind of stoneware similar to that made in Corea and in the southernmost part of China. The surface is not always plain, some parts being wrinkled and others swelled, giving it a curious appearance. Ware made here between 1520 and 1580 is called *Ko-Tamba*. This factory now produces a common ware, glazed with different coloured enamels, for the use of the lower class of people.

49. WATER JAR (*midzu-ire*), of irregular cylindrical form and rudely made ; pale-red ware, covered with a sage-green glaze of irregular thickness ; on the outside vertical scorings. Lacquer lid. Tamba ware, made about 1620. H. 6 in. w. 6¼ in.

208.77.

50. TEA JAR (*cha-ire*) with wide mouth ; red ware, entirely covered

with a brown glaze, mottled with yellow round the lip. *Itoguiri* lines on the bottom. Ivory lid. Tamba ware, made about 1670. H. 2½ in. diam. 2⅞ in.                              209.77.

### SHITORO WARE.

This ware was first made in the period Shoho (1644–47) in a village called Shitoro-mura, in the province of Tôtômi. The trade now consists in tea utensils. The body is composed of red clay, and covered with a glaze containing a small amount of ochre; the name of the factory is impressed, whereas the earlier specimens were marked by engraving with a spatula.

51. INCENSE BURNER (*koro*) in the form of an elephant, with an opening on his back closed by a lid; reddish-brown ware, covered with an irregular glaze, red and brown. Shitoro ware, made at Shitoro-mura, in the province of Tôtômi, about 1670. H. 6¾ in. l. 9¾ in.                              210.77.

### ZEZE WARE.

This ware is produced in the small town of Zeze, near the lake of Omi.

The factory was founded about the Shoho period (1644–47) for the purpose of making tea utensils on a large scale. They consisted of a kind of stoneware, the glaze very strongly resembling the *Ko-Seto.* There is still a small kiln in operation.

52. TEA JAR (*cha-ire*); brownish-grey stoneware, covered inside and out with a brown glaze, mottled with a darker tint. *Itoguiri* lines on the bottom. Ivory lid. Made at Zeze, province of Omi, about 1640. H. 3½ in. diam. 2⅞ in.                              211.77.
53. TEA JAR (*cha-ire*) in the form of a double bulb; grey ware, covered with a pale liver-coloured glaze, mottled with dark brown. *Itoguiri* lines on bottom. Ivory lid. Made at Zeze, province of Omi, about 1700. H. 2½ in. diam. 2⅜ in.
                              212.77.

## ASAHI WARE.

The factory from which this ware emanated was founded in the Shoho period (1644-47), and is situated at Uji, in the province of Yamashiro. The name *Asahi Yaki*, or Asahi ware, is derived from its colour resembling the morning light,* as does also the famous Corean tea bowl distinguished as *Chosen-no-go-hon.* This factory was celebrated from the earliest times for making the vessels in which ground tea was stored.

It is said that Kobori Masakatzu,† son of Kobori Tôtômi-no-Kami, founder of one branch of the tea ceremony, encouraged the manufacturer by honouring him with a seal to be used for marking his productions. At the present time tea jars and tea vases of every description are manufactured here. In the vicinity at Tawara is another factory founded about the same time; its produce consisted mostly of tea pots used in Uji, the centre of the tea-cultivating district in Japan.

Fig. 12.
Asahi.
No. 54

54. TEA BOWL (*cha-wan*); grey ware, covered with a greenish-grey glaze. Mark impressed, *Asa-hi*, " Morning light." [Figure 12.] Asahi ware, made at Uji, province of Yamashiro, about 1700. H. 2⅜ in. diam. 5½ in.                    213.77.

## TAKATORI WARE.

The factory is situated in a village called Sobara-mura, in the province of Chikuzen, where an imitation of Chinese ware had already been made in the periods Onin and Bunmei (1467–86). The most eminent maker is said to have been Hachizo. The ware, for which a red-coloured clay was used, is known as *Ko-Takatori.* The first glaze is rather a light brown, and is marbled by spreading over it another glaze of deep yellow or black. (No. 55.)

* [Ninagawa says that it is so called from the mountain Asahi Yama to the east of Uji.]
† [This distinguished patron of the tea ceremonies died in 1647, aged 69.]

In the period Shoho (1644–47) a clay of light yellowish or greyish-white colour came into use. The glaze used for it contained a small amount of oxide of iron, and, after two or three applications, produced a very fine metallic lustre. This particular ware is distinguished as *Yenshiu Takatori*, which is derived from the name of the above-mentioned Kobori Masakatzu or Yenshiu, who greatly admired it and encouraged its manufacture. (Yenshiu is an abbreviation of Tòtòmi.)

In 1614 a priest made here for the first time statuettes representing the Chinese saint Kanzan.

In 1690 Igarashi Jihei resumed the trade, and it has descended in two families of Takatori and Yama-kuchi, together with the art of manufacturing utensils for the tea ceremony and other articles. (Nos. 56–58.)

55. BARREL-SHAPED TEA JAR (*cha-ire*); chocolate ware, the upper part of outside covered with a bright reddish-brown glaze. *Itoguiri* marks on bottom. Ivory lid. Takatori ware, made at Sobara-mura, province of Chikuzen, about 1520. H. 3⅛ in. diam. 2⅜ in. 214.77.

56. CYLINDRICAL WATER JAR (*midzu-ire*); brown ware, covered with a thin glaze, grey inside, yellowish-brown outside, where it is ornamented with horizontal scorings. Lacquer lid. Takatori ware, made at Sobara-mura, province of Chikuzen, about 1640. H. 6⅛ in. diam. 6¼ in. 215.77.

57. GLOBULAR TEA JAR (*cha-ire*); fine brownish-grey ware, partly covered with a chocolate glaze, with darker lines horizontally disposed ; over the shoulder is a patch of yellowish green glaze. Takatori ware, made at Sobara-mura, province of Chikuzen, about 1690. H. 2 in. diam. 2⅜ in. 216.77.

58. TEA BOWL (*cha-wan*); red ware, covered with a pale greenish-grey glaze, over which, round the lip, is run a glaze of yellowish-brown ; on the sides two storks rudely incised. Two nicks cut out of the foot-rim. Takatori ware, made at Sobara-mura, province of Chikuzen, about 1770. H. 3⅛ in. diam. 4⅛ in. 217.77.

## HAGI WARE.

The origin of the pottery at Hagi, in the province of Nagato, is unknown. At first only the common kind of ware was made there. It is stated that in the period Yeisho, in 1510, the manufacture of tea utensils was commenced; it appears however to have been confined to tea bowls. A century later, a Corean named Rikei, who when in Japan adopted the name of Korai Saiyemon, settled at Hagi, and began by making a kind of faïence. A part of the raised edge at the bottom of each piece made by the Corean is cut out, leaving a space of triangular form. This is a peculiarity common to the pottery imported from Corea. The same occurs in wares made in the Island of Tsushima, and in the provinces of Higo and Satsuma, where the art had also been introduced from Corea. The produce up to the period Shoho is generally called *Ko-hagi*; whereas the articles manufactured by Korai Saiyemon are known by his name. (No. 59.) His descendants of the eighth generation are the present manufacturers.

59. TEA BOWL (*cha-wan*) rudely made; pale-brown ware, covered with a dull salmon glaze, slightly crackled. Two nicks cut in the foot-rim. Made at Hagi, province of Nagato, about 1760 in imitation of the work of Korai Saiyemon, of about 1620 H. 3½ in. diam. 5¾ in. 218.77.

60. TEA BOWL (*cha-wan*) of coarse and irregular make; chocolate ware, covered with a pale greyish glaze, crackled. A nick in the foot-rim. Ko-Hagi ware, made at Hagi, province of Nagato, about 1640. H. 3½ in. diam. 5½ in. 219.77.

## MATSU-MOTO WARE.

This ware was made at Matsu-moto, in the province of Nagato. The factory was founded by Miwa Kiusetsu, a native of the province of Yamato, who settled here, having previously been engaged in an attempt to produce Raku ware. He erected a kiln on the Corean system. His productions were known as Matsu-moto yaki; but, in consequence of their resemblance to Hagi ware, are now distinguished as *Matsu-moto Hagi*. Miwa Kiu-

setsu died in the period Hoyei (1704–11), at the age of more
than eighty years. The works are kept up by his descendant
Tozo, of the seventh generation.

61. TWO SHALLOW BOWLS for fruit (*sara*), each on three feet ; dark-
    grey ware, covered with opaque pale-grey glaze, with tinges of
    pink and light blue, crackled. Made by Miwa Kiusetsu, at
    Matsumoto, in the province of Nagato, about 1710. Diam.
    6⅜ in.                                                   220.77.
62. BOWL (*hachi*); brown ware, covered with a greyish-buff glaze,
    showing the paste through in specks ; slightly ribbed on the
    outside. Made at Matsumoto, province of Nagato, about 1770.
    H. 5 in. diam. 15⅜ in.                                   221.77.

## IDSUMO WARE.

This ware was made in the village of Matsuyé, in the province of Idsumo, the kiln having been established in the period
Manji (1658–60) by Gombei, a potter of Hagi, in the province of
Nagato. As he used the Hagi clay, the products had much of
the character of the true Hagi ware. (No. 63.) About the
periods Kiôwa and Bunkwa, *i.e.* in the beginning of the nineteenth
century, a skilful manufacturer of the name of Hanroku received
on several occasions orders from Matsu-daira Idsumo-no-kami,
prince of the province, and one of the distinguished men of the
tea ceremonies, to make imitations of the ancient ware. He
succeeded in producing some very tasteful specimens of his art,
which are even now much valued by the tea-drinkers. (No. 64.)
The ware from this kiln, which is now known as Rakuzan-yama,
consists not only of tea utensils, but also of ware for general
use preserving the earlier characteristics.

63. TEA BOWL (*cha-wan*); pale-brown ware, partly covered with an
    opaque yellowish-buff glaze, and green on one side. Made
    by Gonbei, at Matsuye, province of Idsumo, about 1660.
    H. 2⅞ in. diam. 5½ in.                                   222.77.
64. TEA BOWL (*cha-wan*); brown ware, covered with a green glaze
    passing into yellow and minutely crackled ; flattened in on two
    sides. Made by Hanroku, at Matsuye, province of Idsumo, in

1803, in imitation of the earlier ware of that place.  H. 3 in.
diam. 5⅞ in.                                    223.77.

### FUJINA WARE.

As this ware is also made in Matsuye, it is commonly called

Idsumo yaki.   The factory was founded by Prince
Fumai.   A large proportion of the ware is composed of
a soft but very tough clay, and coated with a fusible
glaze of different colours.   It is sometimes decorated
under the glaze.    In later years, conformably to an
order of Kobori Masakatzu, a distinguished tea-drinker,
a decoration in imitation of the Satsuma ware was commenced, and is now carried on on an extensive scale.

Fig. 13.
Fujina.
No. 66.

65. QUADRANGULAR WATER VESSEL (*midzu-ire*) with a flat bar across
the mouth as a handle ; dull-red stoneware, covered with a thin
red glaze, over which has been spread a thick sage-green glaze,
reaching nearly to the bottom, and having on each face a streak
of dark brown and grey.  At each angle vertical furrows; inside
a pearly-grey glaze.  Lacquer lid in two pieces.  Fujina ware,
made at Matsuye, province of Idsumo, about 1820.  H. 7¼ in.
w. 6⅜ in.                                    224.77.

66. PAIR OF PRICKET CANDLESTICKS (*shoku-dai*) ; grey ware, covered
with a pale sea-green glaze; the base bell-shaped.  Mark
impressed, *Un-yei*, maker's name.  [Figure 13.]  Fujina ware,
made at Matsuye, province of Idsumo, about 1830.  H. 15½ in.
                                             225.77.

67. TRAY (*sara*) in the form of a fan-mount, on three small feet, glazed
in three irregular bands, white, buff, and liver-coloured, and
ornamented with flowers in white slip, with brown leaves.
Fujina ware, made at Matsuye, province of Idsumo, about
1830.  L. 6⅜ in.                             226.77.

68. CYLINDRICAL TEA BOWL (*cha-wan*) ; drab ware, covered with a
white crackle glaze, and painted in enamel colours with gilding;
chrysanthemums and other flowers ; border of hexagons and
quatrefoils.  Imitation of Satsuma ware, made by order of
Kobori Sochiu, at Matsuye, province of Idsumo, about 1840.
H. 3⅜ in. diam. 4⅜ in.                       227.77.

69. FIRE VESSEL (*hi-ire*), double bulb shape ; pale-grey ware, covered

with a crystalline brown glaze, mottled ; edge of foot divided into three portions. Fujina ware, made at Matsuye, province of Idsumo, about 1840. H. 3½ in. diam. 4⅝ in.     228.77.

70. JAR-SHAPED FIRE VESSEL (*hi-ire*); buff ware, the outside and lip coloured yellow, over which is a brilliant brownish-red glaze; on the shoulder, five loop handles. Fujina ware, made at Matsuye, province of Idsumo. H. 4¾ in.     229.77.

71. SAKÉ POT (*saké-tsugi*) with a spout and two loops on the top, through which is passed a twig handle ; pale-buff pottery, covered with a pale-yellow glaze, crackled, with a splash of green on the cover ; on one side is sketched in dark outline a gourd plant, with the name of the artist, *Gen-sho-sai ho-in*, " the hoin (a religious title) Genshosai." Mark stamped, *Un-yei*, maker's name. [Figure 13.] Fujina ware, made at Matsuye, province of Idsumo, 1840. H. 4⅞ in.     230.77.

## AKAHADA WARE.

This ware is from a kiln at Kōriyama, in the county of Soishimo, province of Yamato. Its origin dates from the period Shoho (1644–47). For many years tea utensils only were made ; at present the manufacture is extended to all kinds of vessels used in eating and drinking. The ware has the general appearance of Hagi yaki, but the character of the clay is different. The earlier productions are engraved by means of a bamboo spatula with the word *Aka-hada*, partly in Chinese, partly in Japanese characters [as in fig. 14, but not stamped]. From the time of Kobori Masakatzu the mark was changed, and a seal used bearing the word *Aka-hada*, written entirely in Chinese. The mark given above [figure 14] was used in specimens of more recent manufacture, and was made for the most part in accordance with orders received from the prince of the province.

Fig. 14.
Akahada.
No. 72.

72. CYLINDRICAL FIRE VESSEL (*hi-ire*) on three small feet ; buff ware covered with a thick whitish glaze, crackled. Mark stamped in a curved gourd-shaped panel, *Aka-hada*, name of the factory. [Figure 14.] Akahada ware, made at Kōriyama, province of Yamato, 1840. H. 3¼ in. diam. 4½ in.     231.77.

E

73. INCENSE BOX (*ko-go*) in the form of Hotei, the god of content-
    ment ; pale-brown ware, with dark-brown glaze on the cloak.
    Mark stamped in a gourd-shaped panel, *Aka-hada*. [Figure 14.]
    Akahada ware, made at Koriyama, province of Yamato, about
    1840.  H. 2⅜ in.                                    232.77.

MINATO WARE.  ·

The factory is situated near the town of Sakai in the province
of Idsumi.  Its origin is of great antiquity, and it is even said
that Giyogi, the inventor of the potter's wheel, was the first
to commence working here.  The ware made in the period
Tensho (1573–91) was a kind of biscuit, and was very
brittle.  Afterwards a thin glaze was introduced similar
to that on the Cochin-Chinese ware, and at the present
time both biscuit and glazed wares are produced.  In
the same period Hachita Gensai founded a pottery here,
where he made earthenware fire-holders for use at tea
ceremonies.  They are known as *Gensai yaki*, and are
similar in appearance to the Minato yaki.  This factory,
however, has been discontinued.  Other kilns are known to have
existed, but their locality has not been determined.

Fig. 15.
Minato.
No. 74.

74. ASH BOWL (*hai-ki*), used in the tea ceremonies; biscuit-like yellow
    ware, unglazed, showing marks of the wheel, and ornamented
    with three impressed lozenges of lattice work.  Mark stamped,
    *Minato yaki*, " Minato ware."  [Figure 15.]  Made near Sakai,
    province of Idsumi, about 1770.  Diam. 7¼ in.      235.77.

YANAGAWA WARE.

This is a species of terra-cotta, from a factory in the town of
Yanagawa in the province of Chikuzen, founded in the period
Keicho (1596–1615), and still in operation.

75. ASH BOWL (*hai-ki*), on three small feet, with edge curved in-
    wards ; biscuit-like yellow ware, with tinges of brown, and
    with scratched and impressed patterns  Made at Yanagawa,
    province of Chikuzen, about 1820.  Diam. 13 in.    234.77.

76. ASH BOWL (*hai-ki*), on three small feet, with edge curved inwards; stone-coloured ware, covered with a bluish-grey glaze; on the edge incised hatching, and leaves applied in white. Made at Yanagawa, province of Chikuzen, in 1841. Diam. 13 in.
233.77.

## TOYO-URA WARE.

The factory at which this ware is produced is supposed to have been founded in the Kiôho period (1716–35). It is situated at the foot of the hill of Toyo-ura yama, in the province of Nagato. The trade was originally in ash bowls for use at the tea ceremonies, but is now in an inferior ware with a white glaze, for domestic use. The works are small and but little known.

Fig. 16.
Toyo-ura.
No. 77.

77. ASH BOWL (*hai-ki*); pinkish-yellow biscuit-like ware, unglazed, with three black marks on the sides. Mark stamped, *Toyo-ura yama*, the name of the factory. [Figure 16.] Made at Toyo-ura yama, province of Nagato, 1846. Diam. 7½ in.
236.77.

## RAKU WARE.

The manufacture of this ware was introduced in the period Yeiroku (1558–69), by a Corean named Ameya, who settled in the old capital Kiôto. He commenced work with a clay found at Juraku, a district of Kiôto, on which account the ware might better be called Juraku yaki; but Taiko Hideyoshi having honoured the manufacturer, the son of Ameya, with a gold seal on which was engraved the character "Raku," signifying "enjoyment," it has been called *Raku yaki*. Ameya's work is very rare and much appreciated. He died in 1574, leaving a son named Tanaka Chojiro, who followed his father's trade; and his descendant of the eleventh generation now carries on the business. The ware, which is of a common black description, with a glaze containing lead, consists of small vases, each being separately baked; and the trade was chiefly in tea bowls, shaped

E 2

by hand alone, although other things were made—such as incense holders and water pitchers. It has always been in great favour in the tea ceremonies, not only on account of its artistic appearance, but also from its great smoothness and its speciality for keeping the water hot. The son of Ameya or Chojiro, who is known as the first of this family, used for marking the tea bowls the gold seal given him by Taiko ; but in the time of the second Chojiro this seal was lost, after which each manufacturer used his own.

The tenth generation, named Tan-niu, was honoured with a seal by the prince of Kii, of the family of the Shogun. Another seal, with the character of Raku, was occasionally used, impressed in a double circle.

In the collection are included pieces made by each generation, except the first ; their names are as follows :

       1. Chojiro.
       2. Chojiro.
       3. Do-niu.
       4. Ichi-niu (or Sahei).
       5. So-niu.
       6. Sa-niu.
       7. Cho-niu.
       8. Toku-niu.
       9. Riyo-niu.
      10. Tan-niu.
      11. Kichizayemon (the present maker).

No. 88 was made by a sword connoisseur called the Honnami Ko-idsu, who died in 1637. He was a great admirer of Raku ware, and himself erected a kiln; but his productions, though similar to the true ware, are somewhat harder. It is much favoured by the tea-drinkers.

Fig. 17.  Raku.

A native of Kiôto named Hirai Ikkan, a maker of a peculiar kind of cardboard work, the art of which had descended to him from an ancestor, succeeded

last year (1875) in making an imitation of the old Raku yaki by
pasting together numerous layers of thin paper and covering them
with lacquer. These imitations will stand hot water as well as the
Raku bowls; and it was considered that a specimen of it would
be an interesting addition to the Collection. (No. 89.)

78. TEA BOWL (*cha-wan*), irregular cylindrical form; dark ware covered
with a deep-brown glaze. Made by the 2nd Chojiro, about
1630. H. 3⅜ in. diam. 3¼ in.                                  237.77.
79. TEA BOWL (*cha-wan*); coarse yellow ware, covered with a gritty
glaze of a brilliant red. Mark impressed, *Raku*, " Enjoyment."

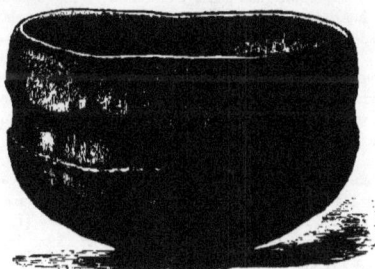

Fig. 18. Tea Bowl, Raku ware. No. 83.

[Similar to figure 17.] Made by the 3rd Chojiro [Do-niu], about
1650. H. 2⅞ in. diam. 5⅛ in.                                  238.77.
It is possible that this specimen and the last may have been
transposed.
80. CYLINDRICAL TEA BOWL (*cha-wan*); coarse ware, covered with a
thick dark bottle-green glaze, somewhat speckled. Made by
the 4th Chojiro [Ichi-niu], about 1690. H. 3½ in. diam. 4⅜ in.
239.77.
81. TEA BOWL (*cha-wan*) with rounded base and small foot-rim; dark
greenish-black ware, thinly glazed and granular. Made by the
5th Chojiro [So-niu], about 1710. H. 3 in. diam. 4½ in.
240.77.

82. TEA BOWL (*cha-wan*); rudely made ware, covered with a reddish glaze. Made by the 6th Chojiro [Sa-niu], about 1730. H. 3¼ in. diam. 4½ in.    241.77.

83. TEA BOWL (*cha-wan*); rudely made, with small foot-rim; pale-red ware, covered inside and partially outside with a yellowish-red glaze; broad scoring on the sides. Mark stamped, *Raku*, "Enjoyment." [Figure 17.] Made by the 7th Chojiro [Cho-niu], about 1750. H. 3¼ in. diam. 3¾ in. [Figure 18.]
    242.77.

84. TEA BOWL (*cha-wan*), hemispherical form, resting on a small raised foot; rudely made pale ware, covered with a deep yellowish-brown glaze; irregular scoring inside and out, and an inscription painted in red, apparently a verse. Made by the 8th Chojiro [Toku-niu], about 1770. H. 4 in. diam. 4⅛ in.
    243.77.

85. CYLINDRICAL TEA BOWL (*cha-wan*); rudely made pale soft ware, covered with a thick rich brown glaze, speckled with white. Mark stamped, *Raku*, "Enjoyment." [Figure 17.] Made by the 9th Chojiro [Riyo-niu], about 1790. H. 3¼ in. diam. 4½ in.
    244.77.

86. TEA BOWL (*cha-wan*); rudely made, covered with red and green glazes arranged in large patches, on which plants are incised and gilt. Mark stamped, *Raku*, "Enjoyment." [Figure 17.] Made by the 10th Chojiro [Tan-niu], about 1810. H. 3¼ in. diam. 4⅜ in.    245.77.

87. CYLINDRICAL TEA BOWL (*cha-wan*), irregular in form; rough stone-coloured ware, thickly covered with a brilliant black glaze. Two marks stamped, *Raku*, "Enjoyment" [figure 17], and *Sen-raku yen sei*, "Made at the Senraku garden." [Figure 19.] Made by the 11th Chojiro [Kichizaye-mon], about 1840. H. 3¼ in. diam. 4⅜ in.    246.77.

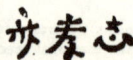

Fig. 19.    Fig. 20.
Raku Ware.    Raku Ware.
No. 87.    No. 89.

88. CYLINDRICAL TEA BOWL (*cha-wan*) of thin substance, but rudely made, and with sharp edges and slight foot-rim; pale-buff ware, irregularly covered with a dark-brown glaze. Made by the Honnami Koidzu, an amateur of Kiôto, about 1630. H. 3⅛ in. diam. 5 in.    247.77.

89. CYLINDRICAL TEA BOWL (*cha-wan*) of papier-mâché, entirely covered with rich dark-brown lacquer ; three nicks in the foot-rim. Mark painted in red, *Shi-ko sai,* " The study of Shiko." [Figure 20.] H. 3¼ in. diam. 4¾ in. 248.77.

## ŌHI WARE.

This ware is the produce of a kiln at Ōhi-machi, on the boundary of the town of Kanazawa in the province of Kaga. It was founded on the Raku system, in 1680, by a man named Chozayemon, and was encouraged by some of the tea-drinkers, such as Senso, Soshidsu, and others. Although the ware produced is similar in kind to the Raku, it has not quite the same appearance, being somewhat redder and denser; the glaze is very smooth, and of a yellowish-red, with a lustre similar to the foreign platina lustre. At one time a mark resembling a whirlpool was in use. The ware made by the fourth Chozayemon, a descendant of the founder, bears a seal with the character of Ōhi. [Figure 21.] The inhabitants of the village are now nearly all engaged in pottery-making, each house possessing a kiln, and making ordinary ware for domestic use.

Fig. 21. Ōhi.

Fig. 22. Ōhi. No. 91.

90. TEA BOWL (*cha-wan*) ; rudely made, pale ware, covered with a bright yellow-brown glaze. Made at Ōhi-machi, province of Kaga, about 1790. H. 2⅞ in. diam. 4¼ in. 249.77.
91. CYLINDRICAL TEA BOWL (*cha-wan*); soft reddish ware, covered with a bright-brown glaze, irregular in tint ; round the outside of lip a band of impressed circles. Mark scratched, *Sen-ki,* maker's name. [Figure 22.] Made at Ōhi-machi, province of Kaga, about 1820. H. 3⅞ in. diam. 4⅛ in. 250.77.

## HORAKU WARE.

The factory from which this ware emanated was also erected on the Raku system, in 1820, by a man named Toyosuké, and is

situated near the town of Nagoya in the province of Owari.
Latterly, a production, the outside of which is covered with
lacquer, and decorated with lacquer-painting, has come into
favour. It is called Toyosuké, after the inventor, and eating
and drinking utensils are made of it for daily use, but are not
used at the tea ceremonies.

[The specimen of this ware mentioned in the list is wanting.]

### [ASAKUSA] RAKU WARE.

In the Middle Ages, Haridsu, a lacquer worker in Kiôto, was
in the habit of covering the Raku ware made by himself with a
unique and splendid lacquer, incrusted with figures of flowers,
insects, etc.

This art was afterwards followed by a native of Kiôto named
Mi-ura Kenya, who settled at Asakusa, in
the northern part of Tokio, some twenty
years ago. He is now of great age, and
his later work does not appear to equal his
earlier productions, which are very correct
and natural. (No. 92.) He has been succeeded in the trade by Kozawa Benshi,
about whom more information will be given. Another potter
named Kenzan, has given some attention to this branch of work.

Fig. 23. Raku. No. 92.

92. BOWL (*hachi*); yellow ware, covered with a dark-green glaze, over
which are scattered large white flowers with yellow centres.
Mark in purple, *Ken nari*, " It is Ken." [Figure 23.] Said
to be made by Mi-ura Kenya, of Kiôto, 1850. H. 4 in. diam.
8 in.                                                     251.77.

This specimen, though ascribed in the Japanese catalogue to Kenya,
does not seem to agree with what is said of that artist's work, which is
stated to be lacquered; it closely resembles Kenzan's work both in
execution and mark.

### [TOKIO] RAKU WARE.

Kozawa Benshi, just mentioned, lives by the bank of the
river Sumidagawa, in Tokio, and has long been engaged in the

manufacture of Raku ware. Latterly he has succeeded in making figures of terra-cotta, after the designs in children's picture-books, with the aid only of bamboo spatulæ and knives ; and by doing so has revived the art already practised by Mi-ura Kenya. It is to be hoped that Mr. Kozawa will be successful should he study the foreign plastic art.

93. SQUARE TRAY of red and black lacquer, inlaid with shells and a small crab in pottery. Made in Tokio, by Kozawa Benshi, 1875. 12¾ in. square. 252.77.

94. ORNAMENT (*okimono*) in the form of a seated figure of a *samurai* in court costume ; white pipe-clay, richly painted in body colours. He holds a closed fan in his right hand and has his left on his hip. Mark impressed, *Ni-pon To-kio to-ko Raku-ho*, " Rakuho, potter of Tokio in Japan." [Figure 24.] Made by Kozawa Benshi, at Tokio, in 1875. H. 4½ in.
253.77.

Fig. 24.
Raku.
No. 94.

95. ORNAMENT (*okimono*) in the form of a seated figure of an old woman looking sedulously on the ground ; white pipe-clay, richly painted in body colours. Mark impressed, same as the last. Made by Kozawa Benshi, at Tokio, in 1875. H. 3¾ in. 254.77.

96. OBLONG BOX of white pipe-clay, covered with minute dots ; round the edge is a gilt cord from which hang six white glazed tassels ; within is the arm of a demon in full relief, green glazed and with gilt claws. This refers to a legend in which Watanabé no Tsuna cuts off the arm of a demon. Made by Kozawa Benshi, at Tokio, 1875. L. 2½ in. 255.77.

### [OSAKA] RAKU WARE.

This is manufactured by a native of the city of Osaka, named Kikko, who is still living. His work is finer and more delicate than other Raku, but is not so tasteful, and consequently not favoured by the tea-drinkers. His common ware is very good.

Fig. 25.
Raku.
No. 97.

97. ORNAMENT (*okimono*) in the form of a seated figure of Fukurokujiu, the god of longevity, holding a hand-screen in

his left hand ; yellow ware, glazed in various colours.   Mark
stamped, *Kitzu-ko* or *Kik-ko,* the maker's name.   [Figure 25.]
Made at Osaka, 1860.   H. 5¼ in.                    256.77.

98. CYLINDRICAL TEA BOWL (*cha-wan*); rough grey ware, covered
with a thick deep-brown glaze, minutely speckled ; on the
sides are engraved circular designs with bars.   Mark stamped,
*Kitzu-ko* or *Kik-ko,* maker's name.   [Figure 25.]   Made at
Osaka.   Modern.   H. 3½ in.                          446.77.

### [DÔHACHI] RAKU WARE.

Another description of Raku ware, made by Takahashi
Dôhachi, in the period of Tempo (1840).   He was himself one of
the tea-drinkers, and attempted an imitation of Raku from two
kinds of clay, red and white.   His works were in good taste, and in
great demand ; his porcelain especially displaying his artistic talent.

99. CYLINDRICAL WATER VESSEL (*midzu-ire*) and cover, on three
small feet, made in imitation of wood ; glazed of a bright
yellowish-brown, on which are white chrysanthemums in relief,
tinted green.   Said to be made by Takahashi Dôhachi, 1830.
H. 6¼ in.                                     257.77.
It is not quite certain whether this is the right specimen, as it is
described in the Japanese list as a "jug."   It somewhat resembles
Kikko's work.

### FUSHIMI WARE.

As stated near the beginning of this description,* Fushimi-
mura in the province of Yamashiro, had been the site of a
pottery at a very remote period.   In the sixteenth century
a manufacturer named Koyemon commenced to make human
figures with plastic clay, and they are still made by the inhabitants of the neighbourhood.   These figures are made in clay
moulds, each part separately, then joined together and painted
with different colours, but not glazed.   (No. 100.)

The unglazed cups or pots used in temples for religious
festivals are also made here.   The trade is carried on in the
neighbouring village of Fukakusa.

* Page 24.

100. ORNAMENT (*okimono*) in the form of a figure of Fukurokujiu, the god of longevity, with an attendant boy ; white clay, painted in body colours ; on the back an inscription signifying, " February, the 3rd year of Bun-roku, wrought by Ko-ye-mon," i.e. A.D. 1594. Made at Fushimi, in 1840, in imitation of the figures of Koyemon. H. 7 in. 258.77.

## IMADO WARE.

At Imado-machi, in the northern district of Tokio, are situated a number of small kilns, where an inferior kind of earthenware for domestic use, and roofing tiles, are made. The manufacture of the mottled ware by mixing red and black or white and black clays, as also a kind of faïence with a very fusible glaze, similar to Raku, dates from a few years back. The origin of these kilns cannot now be ascertained. However, their history and process of manufacture may be ascertained hereafter.

Fig. 26.
Imado.
No. 101.

101. CYLINDRICAL BRAZIER (*hibachi*) with pierced lid ; fine black ware, polished ; round the upper part are five circular openings, and the piercings of the cover form a radiating pattern. Red silk sling for suspension. Mark impressed in an oval, *Gosaburo*, maker's name. [Figure 26.] Imado ware, made at Imado-machi, northern part of Tokio, 1840. H. 8¼ in. diam. 7¼ in. 259.77.

## KIÓTO (SAI-KIYO) FACTORIES,

including Nin-sei ware, Awata ware, Kiyomidzu ware, etc.

A potter of the family of Nono-mura, named Harima-no-Daijio Fujiwara-no-Fujimasa, and entitled Nin-sei, who was living about the periods Shoho and Keian (1644–51), erected kilns in various places ; at Awata, in the eastern part of the city, where they now make Awata ware ; Omuro, in the northern district, where he himself lived ; Mizoro ; Kinkozan, whence a renowned maker, Kinkozan Sohei, derived his title ; Seikanji, where were established the Gojiozaka and Kiyomidzu manufactories ; and Iwa-

kurazan. Since this period many other factories have sprung up—
Narutaki, Takaminé, Yoshida, Oshi-koji, Komatsudani, etc.—but
only two of these are now in existence, viz. Narutaki and Yoshida.

The kiln in Narutaki was erected by a brother of the famous
painter Ogata Korin, named Shinsho, who amused himself in his
leisure hours by making tea utensils in imitation of Ninsei yaki.
The village of Narutaki, where was his residence, is situated at the
foot of the hill of Atago, to the north-west of the Emperor's palace,
or in the direction called " Ken " in Chinese. On this account he
was named " Shisui Kenzan," meaning " beautiful blue hill in north-
west part." He died in 1742, in his eighty-second year, and his
work is much esteemed by the tea-drinkers. (Nos. 111–113.)

The ware known as Ninsei yaki was of two kinds—faïence
and semi-porcelain—and was made with clay from Shigaraki
and other places near the city. The former is now called Awata
ware, and the latter, which is now entirely of porcelain, Kiyomidzu ware. Awata ware is manufactured at Awata, in the
eastern district of Kiôto. The decoration, to within the last six
or seven years, was confined solely to light sketches of Nô, or
ceremonial operatic performances, in a few neutral colours surrounded by a broad gold outline ; lately successful efforts have
been made in ornamenting with designs representing flowers, birds,
or landscapes. (Nos. 106, etc.) There are now twelve families
following the trade ; each family has a kiln, and employs a certain
number of workmen. The best known of these manufacturers
are Kinkôzan Sohei, Tanzan Seikai, Hozan Bunzo, who are
descendants of the original potters; and Taizan Yohei and
Iwakurazan Kichibei, who recently removed to this district from
Mizoro. They make a kind of faïence known as Awata ware.
Tanzan also produces porcelain.

Other descriptions of pottery and porcelain are made at Gojiozaka and Kiyomidzu, a factory started by Otowaya Kurobei and
others, who came from Seikanji-mura, in the period Horeki
(1751–63). (No. 114.) In the beginning of the present century,

Takahashi Dôhachi, Waké Kitei, and Midsukoshi Yosobei commenced to make Sometsuké, or porcelain decorated with cobalt
underneath the glaze, in imitation of Arita ware, from clay imported
from Idsumi-yama, in Arita, in the province of Hizen. Most of the
productions were shaped by hand, and in such good taste that they
have grown into favour with drinkers of tea or saké. (Nos. 115-
118.) The factories have since developed and increased in number,
and there are now eleven families of porcelain makers, of whom
the more prominent are—Kanzan Denshichi, Maruya Sahei, and
Kameya Bunpei; and twenty-one families of faïence makers, including the renowned Dosen and Kisu. There are besides thirteen
families engaged in the manufacture of both porcelain and faïence,
notably Takahashi Dôhachi (second generation), Waké Kitei
(second generation), Kiyomidzu Kichibei, Kiyomidzu Rokubei,
Seifû Yohei, and Mashimidsu Zoroku. To these may be added
Miyata Kameji and Hasegawa Torasuke. Each family has its
own factory independent of others, and but rarely in common.
The total number of factories in this district is twenty-one. Each
is formed of six or seven kilns ranged side by side. The produce
consists chiefly of tea and saké utensils, and occasionally of
ornamental objects, such as flower vases or incense burners. They
mostly belong to the Sometsuké class, but recently different
coloured enamels have been used for their decoration. The
latter, however, is not equal to the former, with the exception of
the work of Kanzan Denshichi, who decorates with gold on red
ground (No. 211), in imitation of Yeiraku (see p. 67); and has
also invented a manner of representing, in porcelain, iron inlaid
with gold.

### NINSEI WARE.

102. INCENSE BURNER (*koro*) in the form of a conch shell;
grey ware with brown spots. It encloses a copper cup
to hold the burning incense. Mark stamped, *Nin-sei*,
maker's name. [Figure 27.] Made by Nonomura
Ninsei, of Kiôto, about 1650. L. 10¾ in.    260.77.

Fig. 27.
Ninsei.

103. GLOBULAR WATER VESSEL (*midsu-ire*) and cover; very rough

buff ware, speckled with fragments of quartz, and partly covered
with a yellow glaze ; the inside glazed grey and crackled.  Mark
stamped, *Nin-sei,* the maker's name.  [Figure 28.]
Made by Nonomura Ninsei, of Kiôto, about 1650, in
imitation of Corean ware.  H. 5⅞ in.          261.77.

104.  CAKE BOX (*kwasi-ire*) of globular shape, in the form of
a precious ball (*hoshi* or *tama*), with pierced cover ;
pale-yellow ware, covered with a crackled glaze ;
three ridges in the form of flames ; zigzag borders in
green and red with gilding ; inside gilt.  Mark stamped,
*Nin-sei,* maker's name.  [Figure 27.]  Made by Nonomura
Ninsei, of Kiôto, about 1690.  H. 4⅜ in.  [Figure 29.] 262.77.

Fig. 28.
Ninsei.

Fig. 29.  Cake Box, Ninsei ware.  No. 104.

105.  INCENSE BOX (*kogo*) in the form of a goose ; pale greyish ware,
covered with a drab glaze, bill and eyes dark-brown.  Mark
stamped in an oval, *Nin-sei,* maker's name.  [Figure 27.]  Made
by Nonomura Ninsei, of Kiôto, about 1690.  L. 3½ in.  263.77.

AWATA WARE.

106. INCENSE BURNER (*koro*) in the shape of a building, with an
    entrance at each side, and surmounted by a platform with
    railings, in the middle of which is a cube with openings at the
    side ; buff ware, enamelled blue and green. Made at Awata,
    about 1720. H. 12⅝ in. 264.77.

Fig. 30. Brazier for warming hands. Awata ware. No. 107.

107. BRAZIER for warming the hands (*shu-ro*) in the form of a *tama*
    or Buddhist jewel ; buff ware, covered with grass-green glaze ;
    various symbols in high relief, rain cloak, hammer of Daikoku,
    purse, etc., partly gilt and touched with red and other colours.
    Made at Awata, about 1790. H. 7⅝ in. diam. 7⅛ in. [Figure 30.]
    265.77.

108. FRUIT TAZZA (*sara*) on tripod foot ; cream-coloured ware, covered
    with a thin glaze, crackled and painted in colours with gilding

inside a garland of fruit on a ground of gold dots; outside
floral bands in gold.  On the foot, scrolls in colours and the
inscription, in a horizontal line, *Ni-pon Kiô-to Kin-ko-zan*

造 山 光 錦 都 京 本 日

Fig. 31.  Awata.  No. 108.

*tsukuru,* " Made by Kinkozan, of Kiôto, in Japan." [Figure 31.]
Made at Awata in 1875.  H. 4½ in. diam. 8¾ in.     266.77.

109. TWO CUPS with handles, AND SAUCERS of European form ; buff
ware, covered with a thin cream-coloured glaze
crackled, and painted in enamel colours with flying
birds and trees in bloom.  Two marks, one painted
in red, *Dai Ni-pon Tan-zan sei,* "Made by Tanzan
of Great Japan" [figure 32]; the other impressed
*Tan-zan,* maker's name.  Made at Awata, 1875.
H. of cups 2½ in. diam. of saucers 5⅜ in.  267.77.

帶 大
山 日
製 本

Fig. 32.
Awata.
No. 109.

110. CIRCULAR CAKE BOX (*kwasi-ire*), porcelain ; on the
cover three heart-shaped panels with photographic
views in brown, on a ground of blue diapers ; the
body has three different views on a similar ground.
Mark in blue, over the glaze, *Tan-zan,* maker's name.  Made
at Awata, 1875.  Diam. 5½ in.     268.77.

### KENZAN WARE.

111. BRAZIER for boiling water (*furo*), on three small feet ; buff ware,
covered with yellow glaze crackled, and painted in colours with
gilding ; branches of a creeper with black, blue, and green
leaves.  Made by Ogata Shinsho (Kenzan), about 1730.  H. 7 in.
diam. 10½ in.     269.77.

112. BOWL (*hachi*), with straight sides ; pale ware covered with a
drab glaze crackled, and boldly painted
in enamel colours with snow-covered
pine-trees.  Mark in brown on a white
panel, *Ken-zan,* maker's name. [Similar
to Figure 33.]  Made about 1730.  H.
4⅜ in. diam. 8⅜ in.     270.77.

Fig. 33.  Awata.  No. 112.

113. CYLINDRICAL FIRE-VESSEL for smokers
(*hi-ire*) ; buff ware, covered with a pale
yellow glaze, crackled and painted in brown : on one side a

bulbous plant, boldly painted ; on the other, two verses, followed by the signature of the maker, *Ken-zan to-in*, and a
seal with the word *sho-ko*, "a lover of antiquity." Mark in
brown, *Ken-zan*, the maker's name. [Similar to Figure 33.]
Made about 1750. H. 2¾ in. diam. 4¼ in.      271.77.

## KIYOMIDZU WARE.

114. CIRCULAR INCENSE BURNER (*koro*), on three small feet ; buff
ware, covered with a cream-coloured glaze crackled ;
painted in green with hexagonal network and with
two heart-shaped panels, containing a dragon and
a monstrous lion in gold.  Mark, in an oval, *Sei-
kan-ji*, the name of the village from which the
potters came who made it.  [Figure 34.]  Said
to be made at Kiyomidzu in 1800.  H. 2⅝ in.
diam. 3 in.      272.77.

Fig 34.
Kiyomidzu.
No. 114.

We give the date as given in the Japanese list, though it does not
seem to agree with the statements in the text.  Ninagawa says
that the potter who used this seal was a contemporary of Ninsei, who
lived in the 17th century.

115. BRAZIER for warming hands (*shiu-ro*) in the form of a seated
figure of Okamé, represented as a very stout woman with long
hair, at the back of which is an opening ; yellow ware, covered
with red and brown glazes and gilt.  Made by the first Dôhachi
at Kiyomidzu, 1820.  H. 8½ in.      273.77.

Takahashi Dôhachi began making pottery in the period Bun-sei
(1818–1829) and lived at Gojo in Kiôto.  About 1836 he went to Taka-
matsu (prov. Sanuki) and to Himeji (prov. Harima) to make further
studies.  He also worked at Momoyama (prov. Yamashiro).  In the
period Ka-yei (1848–1853) he was elevated to the rank of Hokkiô,
after which he assumed the name of Ninami.

116. TWO ORNAMENTAL FIGURES (*oki-mono*) of a cock and a hen ;
pale-yellow ware covered with black lacquer; the feet and
bills yellow, wattles red.  Made by the first Dôhachi at
Kiyomidzu, 1820.  L. 9 in.  [Figures 35, 36.]      274.77.

117. INCENSE BURNER (*koro*), in the form of a fanciful lion, pierced
cover on the back ; coarse ware, entirely covered with gilding.
Made by the first Dôhachi at Kiyomidzu, about 1820.  L. 9¼ in.
H. 6 in.      275.77.

118. SQUARE CUP, yellowish ware, covered with a stone-grey glaze,

F

Fig. 35. Cock. Kiyomidzu ware. No. 116.

Fig. 36. Hen. Kiyomidzu ware. No. 116.

and rudely painted with plants in black.  Mark stamped,
*Dôhachi*, the maker's name.  [Figure 37.]  Made at Kiyomidzu, about 1830.  H. 3¼ in. diam. 4⅝ in.

276.77.

For other specimens of Kiyomidzu ware, see
Nos. 211-214.

No. 118.
YEIRAKU WARE.                              Kiyomidzu.
Fig. 37.

This ware is made in Kiôto.  In past years the
trade consisted only of earthen braziers, called Do-Buro ; but at the
beginning of the 19th century Zengoro Riyozen (the tenth generation) commenced making porcelain.  He was most skilful in repro-
ducing the old ware both of China and Japan, especially in
decorating with designs of ancient coats-of-arms, in gold outline
on a red ground coloured with oxide of iron, a species of decoration
first used in the ornamentation of Chinese porcelain made in the
Chinese period Yeiraku [Yung-lo, 1403-25].  This particular production is called Yeiraku Kinranté, in order to distinguish it
from Nishikité, which is similar to the Arita ware.  Both these
wares derive their name from their decoration resembling that
of brocades.  The Prince of Kii, of the family of the Shogun,
honoured the manufacturer with the title of Yeiraku, which he
adopted as his family name, and even applied to the articles he
made—hence the appellation *Yeiraku Kinranté.*  He is sometimes considered as the first of the family, having adopted the
name of Yeiraku.  Specimens of his work, some of which are of
great value, are in the Collection.  (Nos. 119-121.)  Zengoro
Hozen (the twelfth generation) settled some seventeen or eighteen
years ago at Kutani, in the province of Kaga, and did much
towards encouraging and instructing the manufacturers of that
place in the method of making and decorating porcelain.
(No. 122.)

The present maker (thirteenth generation), by reason of his
great talent, has completely sustained the family fame ; his work

F 2

still outrivals the best productions of the Kutani factory and of
Kanzan, of Kiyomidzu. (Nos. 123 and 124.)

119. VASE-SHAPED WATER VESSEL (*midzu-ire*), yellow ware with
crackled glaze, gilt ornaments in relief; *koi* fishes
leaping out of waves. Lacquer cover. Mark stamped
*Ka-hin shi-riu*, "The branch factory of the river."
[Figure 38.] Made at Kiôto by the 10th Zengoro,
Yeiraku Riyozen, about 1810. H. 6⅞ in. diam. 7⅞ in.

Fig. 38. [Figure 39.] 277.77.
Yeiraku.
No. 119. A gold seal with the inscription *Kahin shiriu* is stated by
Ninagawa to have been given to the 10th Zengoro by the
Prince of Kii, when he went in 1827 to work for him; he
also received from the Prince a silver seal inscribed *Yeiraku.*

Fig. 39. Water Vessel. Yeiraku ware. No. 119.

120. TWO SAUCERS (*sara*); pale-buff ware, with design in relief
covered with a dull-blue glaze; the *koi* fish leaping from

waves, clouds above. The bottom glazed yellow. Mark
stamped, *Yei-raku.* [Figure 40.] Made by the 10th Zengoro,
Yeiraku Riyozen, at Kiôto, about
1810. Diam. 5¼ in. 278.77.

121. SAKÉ CUP (*saka-dzuki*), and its stand
(*dai*), porcelain ; the saucer and
the outside of the cup ornamented
with scrolls, flowers, and phœnixes
in gold on a red ground, imitating
gold brocade (*kinranté*); inside the
cup are the fir, prunus, and bamboo trees (*shochikubai*) painted
in blue. Mark, on the cup, *Dai*

Fig. 40.     Fig. 41.
Yeiraku.    Yeiraku.
No. 120.    No. 121.

*Ni-pon Yei-raku sei*, "Made by Yeiraku of Great Japan"
[Figure 41]; on the stand, a representation of a coin with the
four characters, *Fu-ki chô-mei*, "Riches, honour, and a long life."
[Figure 42.] *Kinranté* ware, made at
Kiôto by the 10th Zengoro, Yeiraku
Riyozen, about 1810. Diam. of cup
2⅝ in., of stand 5⅝ in. 279.77.

122. GLOBULAR INCENSE BURNER (*koro*),
porcelain ; painted in red and green ;
on the body monstrous lions and
sacred pearls ; on the cover scrolls
in gold on a red ground, and with
openings. Mark stamped, *Yei-raku*,
maker's name. [Figure 40.] Made
by the 12th Zengoro, Yeiraku Hozen,
at Kiôto, about 1850. H. 3½ in.

Fig. 42. Yeiraku.
No. 121.
280.77.

123. PAIR OF FLOWER VASES (*hana-ike*) porcelain, decorated in gold
on a bright-red ground ; on the body phœnixes among formal
scrolls ; on the neck and foot geometrical designs. Mark in
gold on a red panel, *Dai Ni-pon Yei-raku sei*, "Made by
Yeiraku of Great Japan." [Figure 41.] *Kinranté* ware, made
by the 13th Zengoro, Yeiraku Tokuzen, at Kiôto, 1875. H.
11¼ in. 281.77.

124. TWO SAKÉ CUPS (*saka-dzuki*), similar in form to European egg
cups ; porcelain, covered outside with a celadon glaze with gilt
borders. Mark in gold *Dai Ni-pon Yei-raku sei*, "Made by
Yeiraku of Great Japan." [Figure 41.] Made by the 13th
Zengoro, Yeiraku Tokuzen, at Kiôto, 1875. H. 2¼ in. 282.77.

## OTO WARE.

This ware is produced in the province of Tosa. The factory was founded during the periods Manji or Kwambun (1658–1673) by a man named Shohaku, who had studied under Ninsei. The present trade consists in various domestic articles of an inferior kind for use in the neighbourhood.

[Ninagawa states that Oto is a place in the town of Kôchi, province of Tosa, and that Shohaku was a Corean potter who came to Japan with Chosogabe Motochika, ruler of the province of Tosa, after the invasion of Corea by Taiko Hideyoshi (1592–98). He first worked with Corean materials, and afterwards discovered and used the clay of Nocha yama near Kôchi. He also states that some say that the potter Ninsei was the pupil of Shohaku.]

125. TEA BOWL (*cha-wan*), light-brown ware, covered with a pale-drab glaze crackled, and painted in bluish-black with symbols, rain cloak, hammer of Daikoku, etc. Oto ware, made in the province of Tosa, about 1800. H. 3⅝ in. diam. 4⅝ in.

283.77.

## AWAJI WARE.

This ware comes from a small factory in the village of Iganomura, in the island of Awaji, opposite Hiogo. The kiln was erected forty years ago, by Kashiu Minpei, a native of the island, who learned the potter's art from Ogata Shiuhei, in Gojiozaka near Kiôto. It is of a very delicate yellow tint, like Awata ware, having a beautiful glaze covered with fine cracks, and carefully painted with more or less transparent enamels. Another kind is of a strongly-baked biscuit, glazed with a very fusible mixture of sand and oxide of lead ; which, by the addition of copper oxide, or certain natural coloured clays, assumes a green, yellow, or brown-red colour. This glaze is so fusible that it cannot be again baked in a muffle after painting. The ware is sometimes known as Minpei yaki, from the name of the founder, whose son Sanpei, is now pursuing the same trade.

126. FLOWER VASE (*hana-ike*), in the form of a section of bamboo ; porcelain, covered with a yellow glaze, and with a bamboo in relief, coloured green ; at the foot a purple sprout. Made by Kashiu Minpei, about 1830. H. 11⅜ in. diam. 4⅞ in.

284.77.

127. SAUCER DISH (*sara*) ; porcelain, with ornaments incised in outline and glazed green and purple, on a Nankin yellow ground ; in the centre a phœnix surrounded by conventional sprigs. Made by Kashiu Minpei, about 1830. Diam. 12¼ in. 285.77.

128. TWO CUPS with straight sides, fluted half way up the body ; porcelain, yellow glazed. Mark in brown of the Chinese period Wan-leih, 1573–1620. [Figure 43.] Made by Kashiu Minpei, about 1830. H. 2 in. diam. 2⅛ in.

286.77.

129. FLOWER VASE (*hana-ike*), with flat expanding mouth in a separate piece, and two small handles in the form of elephants' heads ; creamy ware with crackle glaze, painted in enamel colours with gilding ; on the top phœnixes, on the body peacocks among peonies. Mark in gold, *Ni-pon Awa-ji Ka-shiu San-pei,* "[Made by] Kashiu Sanpei in Awaji, Japan," 1875. [Figure 44.] H. 7½ in. diam. of top 7 in.

| 賀 | 日 |
|---|---|
| 曆 大 | 集 本 |
| 年 明 | 三 淡 |
| 製 苪 | 平 路 |

Fig. 43.  Fig. 44.
Awaji.  Awaji.
No. 128.  No. 129.

287.77.

130. TEA SERVICE, consisting of a gourd-shape tea pot, sucrier and cover, milk jug, and two cups and saucers, all of European shapes ; cream-coloured ware, covered with a thin crackle glaze, and painted in enamel colours with flowers, peonies, pomegranates, etc. Mark in gold, *Ni-pon Awa-ji Ka-shiu San-pei,* "[Made by] Kashiu Sanpei in Awaji, Japan." [Figure 44.] On the saucers *San-pei* only. Date, 1875. H. of tea pot 6½ in., jug 4¾ in., diam. of sucrier 5⅜ in., saucer 4¼ in. 288.77.

## KISHIU WARE.

The factory is situated in Wakayama, in the province of Kii, and is supposed to have been founded 200 years ago. After the reception by the prince of the province of the famous potter

Yeiraku Zengoro, a fresh impulse was given to the art. However, as there was no good clay to be had, its advance was to
a certain extent limited; and at the present day only an inferior
kind of domestic ware is produced. This is generally glazed
with three different enamels of purple, yellow, and blue, giving it
a mottled appearance.

[According to Ninagawa the manufacture of Kishiu ware
dates from the period Bun-kwa (1804-17). In 1827 the wares
were greatly improved by Zengoro Hozen from Kiôto (see
Yeiraku ware, p. 67). The mark used was *Kairaku yen.*
During the period Ka-yei (1848-53) the factory
was removed to Oyama in the same province,
and the wares were inscribed *Nanki oyama.* This
lasted till about 1870. Since then imitations of
Kishiu ware have been made at Tokio by a
subject of the Prince of Kii, which are marked
*San-raku yen.* Still more recently a man named
Miyai Sajuro made pottery of the same kind at Otamura near
Wakayama. These wares all show a gradual decline from the
earlier fabrics.]

Fig. 45.
Kishiu.
No. 131.

131. VASE with wide neck (*hana-ike*), porcelain, with ornaments
     moulded in raised outline, the ground glazed purple; formal
     panels, circles with the seal character for longevity, etc. Mark
     stamped, *Kai-raku yen sei,* "Made at the Kai-raku (mingled
     enjoyment) garden." [Figure 45.] The name of this garden
     is derived from the Chinese classics. Kishiu ware, made at
     Wakayama, province of Kii, about 1800. H. 18½ in. 289.77.

### SATSUMA WARE.

This ware is now made in the village of Nawashirogawa, in the
province of Satsuma. It is known that pottery-making was introduced from Corea in the period Onin or Bummei (1467-86).
At first the manufacture consisted of a kind of stoneware covered
with a glaze mixed with oxides of iron and lead, and occasionally of
a white ware similar to Corean porcelain. In the beginning of the

17th century the tea ceremony having grown in favour, the demand
for tea utensils increased, in consequence of which the manufacturer
turned his attention to the production of tea jars, bowls, water
vessels, and such like necessaries. Imitations of Cochin-Chinese
ware were also made. The kiln is built on the slope of a hill, after
the Corean system, and is of peculiar construction, differing from
that in Arita and other places. It is built singly, and not in a line
as in other factories. It has a length of 150 feet to 200 feet,
and a height of 5 feet in the centre, of a vault-like form. At the
lower end of the kiln is the furnace, or rather the place to commence the firing. The fuel, consisting of dried wood, is thrown
directly into the kiln, the inside of which communicates with
the outer air by means of an opening in the side wall. Saggars
are not used, and in consequence of this and of the irregular
distribution of heat throughout the kiln, great damage occurs
to the ware. Of the many places to which the art of pottery-
making was introduced from Corea, this is the only one at which
the true Corean kiln exists. The finely-crackled ware, well-
known in foreign markets, dates from about A.D. 1592, when
the Prince of Satsuma, Shimadsu Yoshihisa,* a general of the Japanese army, invading Corea, brought home with him a certain number of porcelain makers with their families, who settled first at
Kagoshima and afterwards at Chiusa, in the province of Osumi,
where they made the ware known as *Ko-chiusa.* (Nos. 132, 133.)
Afterwards they moved to Nawashirogawa, near Kagoshima, and
after many experiments succeeded in producing the ware now known
as Satsuma. Until within the last few years they were kept entirely
separate from the Japanese population, intermarriage being prohibited : thus they preserved to a considerable extent their

---

* [This statement appears also in Ninagawa's work. Mr. Nanjio however has
pointed out to me that Yoshihisa had been conquered in 1587, five years earlier,
by Taiko, and made to resign his office to his younger brother Yoshihiro, who
went to Corea, as general of the Japanese army. Mr. Nanjio's opinion is
confirmed by a specimen in the Franks Collection at Bethnal Green, No.
1388 in the catalogue, second edition.]

language and customs.  Since, however, the establishment of the
Central Government they enjoy the same rights and liberties as
other subjects.  They number about 1450, and are all engaged in
pottery-making.  It is said that in A.D. 1630 a Corean named Koyo,
of the family of Boku, found clay in various localities in the
province, and was the first to make the ware decorated with gold
outline.  A good clay was found by him in Nawashirogawa.

Another kind of ware, introduced from Corea, is composed of
a greyish-white clay, decorated by inlaying white clay in such a
manner as to form a design.  (No. 141.)

[Ninagawa states that, according to Zorioku, coloured decoration was not introduced until the period Bun-kwa, 1804–17.
Other authorities give a somewhat earlier date.]

132. INCENSE BURNER (*koro*), four-sided, on four small feet; cream-
coloured ware, covered with a thin crackle glaze; on each side
is a growing flower in natural colours with gilding.  Ko-chiusa
ware, made at Chiusa in the province of Osumi, about 1660.
H. 2¼ in.                                                290.77.

133. VASE to hold a tea ladle (*shaku-tadé*); pale-yellow ware with
transparent crackle glaze, painted in colours with gilding; on
the body are scattered symbols; round the neck and foot formal
borders.  Ko-chiusa ware, made at Chiusa, province of Osumi,
about 1690.  H. 6¾ in.                                    291.77.

134. INCENSE BURNER (*koro*), in the form of a tripod vase with two
high handles, the cover surmounted by a lion; white ware,
covered with a creamy glaze crackled; formal decoration,
chiefly in red, green, and gold, with formal borders.  Made at
Nawashirogawa, province of Satsuma, about 1720.  H. 7⅝ in.
[Figure 46.]                                              292.77.

135. WATER VESSEL (*midzu-ire*), in the form of a shallow bucket on
three small feet, with straight bar handle; cream-coloured ware
covered with a thin glaze, minutely crackled; the staves are
represented by bands of brilliant colours with gilding.  Lacquer
lids.  Made at Nawashirogawa, province of Satsuma, about
1800.  H. 6⅞ in. diam. 8⅞ in.                            293.77.

136. ORNAMENT (*oki-mono*) representing a young man seated on a
rock, holding a pencil in his right hand and a leaf in his left;
he is dressed in a flowered robe, and has long black hair falling

on the shoulders ; white ware, covered with a pale creamy glaze crackled, and painted in colours with gilding.   Made at Nawa-shirogawa, province of Satsuma, about 1840.   H. 10 in.

294.77.

137. INCENSE BOX (*kogo*) and cover ; fine pale ware, with creamy glaze

Fig. 46.   Incense Burner.   Satsuma ware.   No. 134.

crackled, and painted in colours with gilding ; the surface divided into gadroons, on which are varied diapers.   Made at Nawa-shirogawa, province of Satsuma, about 1820.   H. 2¼. in.

295.77.

138. PAIR OF FLOWER VASES (*hana-ike*), with cylindrical bodies

spreading lips and flattened globular bases ; cream-coloured ware with thin crackle glaze and painted in colours with gilding ; on the bodies squirrels among vines, on the bases a prunus pattern in white and gold ; formal borders. Mark in red, *Ni-pon Satsu-ma Naka-jima sei,* " Made by Nakajima of Satsuma in Japan." [Figure 47.] 1875. H. 9 in. 296.77.

薩　日

摩　中　本

嶋

製

Fig. 47. Satsuma.
No. 138.

139. GLOBULAR TEA POT (*do-bin*), with three legs and loops for over-arching handle ; reddish ware, covered with a dull greenish-grey glaze, beneath which are incised flying storks filled in with white. Mark stamped, in the seal character, illegible. Made at Nawashirogawa, province of Satsuma, 1840. H. 4¾ in. 297.77.

140. GLOBULAR TEA POT (*do-bin*), with loops for overarching handle ; buff ware, covered with a drab glaze and painted in greenish-grey ; clouds and flying storks. Mark stamped, in the seal character, illegible. Made at Nawashirogawa, province of Satsuma, 1840. H. 4⅛ in. 298.77.

141. BOWL WITH COVER (*kamé*) ; grey stone ware, with patterns incised in outline, horizontal bands of lozenges, cinquefoils, etc., filled in with white clay and glazed. Made at Nawashirogawa, in the province of Satsuma, 1870. H. 15¾ in. diam. 15 in. 299.77.

142. FLOWER VASE (*hana-ike*), with globular body and wide mouth ; yellow ware, covered with a thin glaze crackled, and painted in greenish-brown with horizontal lines and bands of hatching, herring-bone pattern, and formal scrolls. Made at Nawashirogawa, province of Satsuma, 1870. H. 10 in. 300.77.

143. GLOBULAR TEA POT (*do-bin*), with loops for overarching handle ; buff ware, covered with a bright reddish-brown glaze. Made at Nawashirogawa, province of Satsuma, 1870. H. 4⅛ in. 301.77.

### YATSU-SHIRO WARE.

This ware is made at the village of Shirno Toyohara, near the town of Yatsu-hashi, in the province of Higo, where the factory was founded at the period Kwanyei or Shôho (A.D. 1624–47) for the purpose of producing ware similar to the Satsuma. It is of a hard porcelain, composed of grey clay, and decorated by inlaying white clay in a small design. It is so fine and in such good

Fig. 48. Flower Vase. Yatsu-shiro ware. No. 145.

taste as to meet with universal approval. Unfortunately the art has perished with the maker, and such fine results cannot now be obtained. However, we hope to encourage its restoration.

144. OVIFORM JAR (*kamé*); grey glazed porcelain, ornamented with

vertical lines, incised and filled in with white. · Mark impressed
not deciphered. Yatsushiro ware, made in the province of
Higo, about 1720. H. 16¼ in.    302.77.

145. FLOWER VASE (*hana-ike*), in the form of a wide-necked bottle,
with globular body and two dragons' heads as handles ; brown
stoneware, glazed, with ornaments incised in the paste, and filled
in with white clay, with blue details on a grey ground ; storks
flying among clouds. Yatsushiro ware, made in the province of
Higo, 1770. H. 8⅞ in. [Figure 48.]    303.77.

146. WALL VASE for flowers (*hana-ike*), barrel-shaped, chocolate
ware, glazed and crackled, ornamented with growing water-
plantains, and a band of Greek fret in white on a grey
ground. Bronze lining. Mark stamped, *Boku*, "a
tree." [Figure 49.] Yatsushiro ware, made in the
province of Higo, about 1800. H. 7 in.    304.77.

Fig. 49.
Yatsu-shiro.
No. 146.

147. SHALLOW TEA BOWL (*cha-wan*), fine chocolate ware,
covered with a greenish-grey glaze, crackled and ornamented inside with a band of white flowers, outside
a broad wavy band of white. Yatsushiro ware, made
in the province of Higo, 1820. H. 1⅞ in. diam. 4¼ in.    305.77.

This appears to be an imitation of Mishima ware, which is said to
be of Corean origin.

### SOMA WARE.

Soma ware, made at Naga-mura in the province of Iwaki, is a
kind of stoneware, decorated in black with a vigorously-sketched
running horse, supposed to have been painted first by Kano
Naonabu, a distinguished artist who was living in A.D. 1670. The
ware derives its name from the family name of a prince of the
province, and as the older ware bears his coat-of-arms, it is
probable that it was made by his order. The decoration of the
horse was not used until the time of his successor.

148. TEA BOWL (*cha-wan*), of peculiar make, as though cut and riveted
in three places in the edge ; yellow ware, thinly glazed and
speckled ; in the bottom, and outside, is a running horse faintly
outlined in brown. Soma ware. Made about 1840. H. 2⅞ in.
diam. 4¼ in.    306.77.

149. CYLINDRICAL FURNACE (*konro*), with an opening on one side for

the fire, and a pierced disc inside on which to rest a kettle ;
rough grey ware, thinly glazed, and sketchily painted with a
herd of horses galloping.  Soma ware.  Made about 1840.
H. 10 in. diam. 5½ in.                                      307.77.

150.  TEA POT (*kiu-su*), with straight hollow handle, and spout at right
angles to it ; grey glazed ware, with a herd of galloping horses
outlined in grey.  Probably belonging to the preceding specimen.
Soma ware.  Made about 1840.  H. 3⅝ in.              308.77.

This form of tea pot was not introduced into Japan until the time of
Yoshimasa Ashikaga, 1449–1471.

## KUTANI WARE.

This ware derives its name from a place called Kutani-mura,
in the province of Kaga, where the clay from which it is made is
found.  Another supposition, which however is incorrect, is that
it received the name Kutani, meaning nine valleys, from the fact
that there are nine valleys in the vicinity of the factory.  Its origin
dates from about the seventeenth century, and the factory is said
to have been founded by a subject of the Prince of Daishoji, named
Tamura Gonzayemon, who had studied the Hizen process of
porcelain-making.  From an examination of his work, which is a
description of *Sometsuké* gilded on the edge, it would appear that
he had undoubtedly studied the art introduced from China by
Gorodayiu Go-Shonsui of Hizen (see p. 85).  Since then progress
has taken place, and glazes of deep green, light purple, and yellow
hues came into use.  In the meantime Kuzumi Morikagé, a most
talented painter, settled in Kaga, and strove to assist the porcelain
makers in the promotion of their art; and it is in consequence of
his success that Kutani ware is known throughout the country.
About the year 1650 a man named Gotô Saijiro erected a. kiln
in Kutani, and proceeded to manufacture a ware with a red ground
decorated with gold outline.  The ornamentation was much
admired by the Prince of Kaga, named Komatsu Dainagon, who
on several occasions ordered the making of articles decorated in
this style, some of which are still extant and of great value.
Tsunayoshi, the Taikun of the fifth generation, also gave en-

eouragement to the manufacturer. After that time the factory declined considerably, and in the period Temmei or Kwansei (A.D. 1781–1800) scarcely any fine work could be procured. Some ten years later, in the period Bunkwa (A.D. 1804–17), a man of the name of Yoshidaya erected a kiln at Yamashiro-mura, and made great efforts to restore the ancient manufacture, while forty years ago a porcelain painter called Shozo resumed the art of painting practised by Morikagé or Saijiro, etc. There has lately been a great advance in the trade, and there exist now some ten kilns at Terai-mura and at Kanazawa-cho, in the counties of Yenuma and Nomi. The Kutani kiln, however, is not a large one, and is some distance from the place where the clay is found, namely Kutani-mura. The village of Kutani is situated in a mountainous region where the snow lasts until June or July, and is therefore unsuitable for the establishment of a pottery. Fresh progress was made when seventeen years ago the porcelain maker Yeiraku, already mentioned, visited the place, and like Shozo and Yuzan, taught the workmen the method of ornamentation called *Kinranté* (see p. 67).

The clay from Kutani is of rather a dark-red colour; hence the ware made from it has a uniform tint. That used for the dark-grey ware comes from elsewhere. A thin, translucent, and perfectly white ware is brought here from many parts, more especially from Arita, for the purpose of decoration. This latter ware is in great favour with the people, but the amateur prefers the original Kutani ware of dark-red and greyish-white colour. The present prominent manufacturers are Yuzan, Shoro, Shigeharu, Kichizô, and Hekizandô.

151. SHALLOW BOWL (*hachi*); coarse porcelain, painted in purple, green, and yellow, with black outlines; in the centre a medallion with bamboo and pine trees on a yellow ground with black dots, surrounded by a band of green, lozenge pattern; edge of purple graining. Mark in black on a square panel, *Fuku*, "Happiness." [Similar to figure 50.] Kutani ware, made about 1620. Diam. 16½ in.                          309.77.

152. SQUARE DISH (*sara*) ; coarse porcelain, painted in yellow, green, and purple ; in the middle peonies on a yellow ground speckled with black ; green border with four yellow panels enclosing bamboos. Mark in black on a green panel, *Fuku*, "Happiness." [Similar to figure 50.] Kutani ware, made about 1620. W. 9 ⅝ in. 310.77.

Fig. 50.
Kutani,
No. 151.

153. TWO SAUCER DISHES (*sara*), with shaped edges ; porcelain ; inside are four medallions with coloured flowers and scrolls ; the space between covered with cross hatching in red ; outside, three similar medallions with red network between them. Kutani ware, made in imitation of Chinese porcelain, about 1770. Diam. 5¾ in.

311.77.

154. CIRCULAR CAKE BOX (*kwasi-ire*); porcelain, painted in enamel colours with gilding and silvering ; on the cover a circular medallion with a formal flower, surrounded by a floral scroll in silver on a deep-green ground ; round the edges of the cover and upper part of the body a band of panels of key pattern in silver, on green and red grounds alternately ; the lower part dark green, and foot-rim silvered. Kutani ware, made about 1770. Diam. 6⅞ in. 312.77.

155. PAIR OF FLOWER VASES (*hana-ike*) ; porcelain, painted in red with rich gilding ; on the body chrysanthemums, peonies, etc., on a gold ground ; on the neck and base, scrolls in gold on a red ground. Mark in red in a circle, *Dai Ni-pon Ku-tani Yu-zan dô sei*, "Made at the Yu-zan Hall at Kutani, in Great Japan." [Figure 51.] Made by Yuzan in 1875. H. 6¾ in.

313.77.

大 內 大
友 日 海 日
山 本 吉 本
堂 九 造 九
製 谷 製 谷

Fig. 51.
Kutani.
No. 155.

Fig. 52.
Kutani.
No. 156.

156. PAIR OF FLOWER VASES (*hana-ike*), with wide mouths and ring handles, porcelain, painted in red with gilding ; round the body a three-clawed dragon among clouds ; at the mouth and foot a band of gilt scroll work on a red ground. Mark in gold in a circle near the base, *Dai Ni-pon Ku-tani Uchi-umi Kichi-zô sei*, "Made by Kichizô Uchiumi, at Kutani in Great Japan" [figure 52] ; on the bottom a square

G

seal in red, *To-zan no in*, " Seal of Tozan." [Figure 53.] Made
in 1875. H. 16 in.                                        31477.

## BANKO WARE.

Fig. 53. Kutani.
No. 156.

In the period Sho-o or Manji (1652–60), a
man named Banko Kichibei established a kiln
in the village of Koume-mura, on the boundaries
of Tokio, which was considered as a branch of
the Kutani factory in the province of Kaga. The
ware from this kiln, the character and ornamentation of which resemble in some degree the Satsuma ware, are now
known as Yedo Banko. (Nos. 157–159.) This manufactory has
been discontinued, and the articles going by the name of Banko
ware in foreign markets are made at Kuwana, Yokka-ichi, and
the neighbouring district in the province of Isé.

The Kuwana factory was founded thirty years since by a porcelain maker named Yiusetsu, a native of the village of Obuké, near
Kuwana, who assumed the name of Banko. He is still living,
but is too old to work. The produce consisted of a peculiar kind
of stoneware, generally unglazed. The character of the ware,
together with the method of manufacturing it, is stated in detail
in the Official Catalogue of the Japanese Section of the Philadelphia
Exhibition. (Nos. 160–164.)

Hashimoto Chiuhei, a native of the village of Kawasaki, in the
province of Shimodsuké, studied this branch of manufacture with
Banko Yiusetsu, and in later years successfully established a
kiln in his native place, where he produces a similar ware from
materials found in the vicinity. His work, however, is not equal
to the original. There was also another kind of Banko ware
called Banko celadon, which is very brilliant and unlike the
Chinese. Its manufacture has, however, been discontinued.

[According to Ninagawa, the Banko factory was not established
till the period Hôreki (1751–63), and the ware was made in imitation of the Chinese pottery of the period Wan-leih (1573–1620);

it is known as *Ko-Banko.* Yiusetsu of the Mori family was the
son of a dealer in waste paper, and accidentally found among his
father's stock the receipts for glazing, etc., of the first Banku,
which led him to become a potter. This was a century later.]

### YEDO BANKO WARE.

157. WATER JAR (*midzu-kamé*), widening at the middle ; pale ware,
painted in red, green, and blue, with touches of yellow ; the
decoration consists of four oval panels, with landscapes
surrounded and connected with each other by red bands ;
the intervening spaces filled with inscribed scrolls and
diapers in blue and green. Yedo Banko ware, made by
Banko Kichibei, at Koumemura, near Tokio, about 1690.
H. 12¼ in. diam. 14½ in.                                315.77.

158. FLOWER VASE (*hana-ike*), widening towards the base ; buff ware,
covered with a yellowish glaze crackled,
and painted in red, with temple-like
buildings among clouds ; at the neck
a band of sunk lines, above which a
row of triangular ornaments. Mark
stamped, *Ban-ko*, maker's name.
[Figure 54.] Yedo Banko ware, made
about 1750. H. 8¼ in.    316.77.

| Fig. 54. | Fig. 55. |
|----------|----------|
| Banko.   | Banko.   |
| No. 158. | No. 159. |

159. FAN-SHAPED DISH (*sara*), buff ware,
covered with a dull glaze crackled, and painted in colours, with
a seaside view ; at the corners diapers in red. Mark stamped
in the seal character, with letters in relief, *Ban-ko*, maker's
name. [Figure 55.] Yedo Banko ware, made about 1750. Size
12½ in. by 15¼ in.                                       317.77.

### ISÉ BANKO WARE.

160. OBLONG DISH (*sara*), in four lobes on three small feet ; pale-yellow
ware painted in imitation of Chinese enamel ; in the centre
chrysanthemums and butterflies in brilliant colours on a yellow
ground ; border of fret and diaper patterns in blue and green.
Banko ware, made about 1840.  11⅜ in. by 7¾ in.   318.77.

161. SQUARE DISH (*sara*), with truncated angles and circular centre ;
brown ware, covered with a greyish-green glaze partly crackled ;
across one corner is painted a tree-trunk in brown with red leaves.

Mark stamped, *Ban-ko,* maker's name. Banko ware, made about 1840. W. 4⅜ in. 319.77.

162 TEA POT (*kiu-su*); thin porcelain, moulded with finger and thumb; inside is a wave pattern in slight relief; the outside covered with a turquoise glaze crackled, and painted with a branch of pomegranate in natural colours; loose ring attached to handle; the knob of cover revolves. Marks stamped on the side on a space left unglazed, *Ni-pon Ban-ko,* and in an oval, *Shiba-ta tsukuru,* "Made by Shibata Banko, Japan." [Figure 56.] 1875. H. 4¼ in. 320.77.

163. FLOWER VASE (*hana-ike*); biscuit porcelain, marbled brown and white; on the sides two oviform white panels, with quails, chrysanthemums, etc., enamelled in colours. Mark stamped, *Ni-pon Ban-ko,* and in an oval, *Shiba-ta tsukuru,* "Made by Shibata Banko, Japan." [Figure 56.] 1875. H. 12⅜ in. 321.77.

Fig. 56. Banko. No. 163.

164. VASE for cigars, the lip curling over to form handles on two sides, three small feet in the form of monsters' heads; red unglazed ware; on one side a bunch of peony in enamel colours; on the other an inscription, the characters inlaid in white clay, being a Chinese verse in praise of the peony (*botan*). Mark stamped, *Ni-pon Ban-ko,* and in an oval, *Shiba-ta tsukuru,* "Made by Shibata Banko, Japan." [Figure 56.] 1875. H. 6 in. 322.77.

## HIZEN FACTORIES.

A number of kilns have been erected in various parts of the province of Hizen—Karatsu, Arita, Oknwaji, Mikawaji, Shiro-ishi, Shida, Koshida, Yoshida, Matsugaya, and Kameyama near Nagasaki. Under the heading of Arita are included the kilns of Ichinose, Hirose, Nagawara, Ou-ho, Hokao, Kuromuta, and others. The oldest of all these kilns is that of Karatsu [already mentioned]; where, however, only an inferior kind of ware for domestic use is made. The works at Arita, now the most important centre of the porcelain industry in Japan, were founded shortly after the Karatsu. The ware made at Arita, Okawaji, Shiroishi, Shida, Koshida,

Yoshida, and Matsugaya, together with the produce of the six branch kilns of Arita, is commonly known as Imari ware, a brief history of which will probably be interesting.

The most important stride in the ceramic art of Japan was the introduction of real porcelain-making, under the direction of Gorodayiu Shonsui, a native of Isé, who visited China for the purpose of studying that branch of trade. On his return he settled in the province of Hizen, where he erected several kilns and succeeded in making porcelain decorated with cobalt, from the excellent materials he found in the neighbourhood. The exact locality of his factory has not been determined. A specimen of porcelain made by him in China and marked with his name, thus : " Gorodayiu Go-Shonsui," followed by the character "Tsukuru," meaning "made," is preserved at Nara. Another piece bearing the four characters "Shon-sui Buji," meaning "Shonsui is safe," is supposed to have been sent to his own country for the purpose of informing his friends of his health. In a collection of Chinese poetry is a verse written to him by a Chinaman named Ri-shintei, when he was on the point of leaving China, which event occurred in the eighth year of Sho-toku [Ching-tih] of the Chinese calendar, or A.D. 1513. (Nos. 165–166.)

The village of Arita was formerly called Tanaka-mura, and is situated about fifty miles distant from Nagasaki, in a northern direction. It was here that a Corean named Ri-sanpei first founded a porcelain factory ; since then several porcelain makers have gathered together, and have caused it to be the great centre of the industry. Ri-sanpei was brought over to Hizen after the Corean War (A.D. 1592) by a general of the army under the command of Prince Nabeshima, and was placed at Taku, where he pursued the trade of porcelain-making, but without much success. He then removed to Tanaka-mura, now called Arita, and again made experiments. However, he does not seem to have succeeded until he found a good material at Idsumi-yama, in the county of

Matsu-ura, which was and is used for making the renowned Arita ware.  From the ruins of an old establishment, where he made some experiments, are occasionally dug up pieces of pottery, generally earthenware ; a defective kind of white porcelain known as *Horidashité* (castaway) has also been found, but it is very scarce. A native of Imari, in the same province, named Higashi-shima Tokuzayemon, had learned from a Chinaman who visited Nagasaki, the method of painting with vitreous colours upon the glaze, and, with the assistance of another potter named Gosu Gombei, he succeeded, after making various experiments, lasting over many years.  In the second year of Sho-ho (A.D. 1645), was commenced the export of pieces ornamented with coloured enamels, in gold and silver, etc., in the first place to a Chinaman named Hachikan. Business was then opened with the Dutch market.  The kind of decoration employed at this factory has become its peculiar monopoly, and has been made especially for the foreign market.* (Nos. 167–177.)

The important town of Arita is situated in a valley near the hill of Idsumi-yama, where are to be found embedded in the rock all the materials necessary for the biscuit, for the coating of the ware before glazing, for the glaze, and other purposes.  Hence every manufacturer helps himself without any system, he is under no control, and can bring away at will whatever he requires. Only large pieces convenient for transport are removed, the broken rock being mere waste ; moreover a great squandering occurs in the transport, storage, and preparation.  In order to avoid such waste, the late prince of the province, of the Nabe-shima family, who governed the country before the revolution, appointed an official to act as overseer of the quarrying; further, he set up a gate on the road to the hill to prevent unauthorised persons from entering the quarries.  Such a step had the appearance of being a check on the free trade of the people, but it was really necessary for the preservation of the excellent materials.

* [This is evidently what is known in Europe as "old Japan."]

Since the establishment of the Central Government this controlling system has been abolished, and the waste will probably be greater than before.

In the period Tempo, or about A.D. 1830, a wealthy inhabitant of Arita, named Hiratomi Yojibei, found that the clay from Hirato was much better suited for receiving the glaze, as it dried more quickly than the Idsumi-yama clay, thus saving a great deal of labour. For the same reason a clay from Goto Island is now generally used. Hiratomi was himself an amateur and a good artist. He was an important man at the tea ceremonies, and contributed greatly to the development of the industry by instructing the manufacturer in the method of painting, and by supplying him with designs. It is said that the making of flower vases and of tea cups with saucers was commenced by him. He sold many pieces to foreigners in Nagasaki, all of which were marked with the character of "Sampo," the title he bore. His son, named Sampo, succeeded him, and is pursuing the trade in great prosperity.

In the period Kwambum, or about A.D. 1665, Daté, the prince of Sendai, sent thither a merchant of Tokio, named Imariya Gorobei, to purchase an article made by Tsuji Kizayemon, which was afterwards offered to the Emperor. Since then the maker has been honoured annually by an order from the Court to supply the ware used in the palace, which is a very clear translucent porcelain, with cobalt decoration. The articles for the Emperor's own use, and for that of the imperial family, are ornamented with the chrysanthemum flower, or the imperial coat-of-arms.* Kizayemon's grandson, Kiheiji, has been distinguished with an official name, Hidachi-no-Daijio. He was a celebrated maker, having accidentally discovered the use of saggars. On opening the kiln after the baking was finished, he found that one pot had fallen inside a larger one set on a lower stand ; on breaking away the outer piece, he found to his astonishment a finished

* [See Introduction, page 18.]

production. This suggested to him the use of an outer box or saggar. The article to be baked is placed in the saggar, covered with a lid, and the joint luted so as to seal it hermetically. It is then put in the kiln. When the baking is finished, the saggar has to be broken. This process, which is known as *Gokuhin*, is only used in baking valuable pieces. In the common process, called *Boshi-iri* the joint of the saggar is not luted. Tsuji Katsuzô, a descendant of Kiheiji, is one of the distinguished manufacturers of the present day, and is especially skilled in piercing porcelain. (No. 186.)    He also receives employment from the Imperial Court.

The exhibits from Arita have been prepared by a local company called Koransha, the more prominent members of which body are Tsuji Katsuzô, Fukami Suminosuké, both very distinguished makers in Japan, and a merchant named Tedzuka Kamenosuké. The president of the company is Fukagawa Yeizayemon. This company made great exertions to procure a creditable display of their produce, and to bring before the notice of foreigners the progress effected in the short space of a year since the Vienna Exhibition. Their efforts were crowned with success, and their contribution proved most attractive. The total number of houses in Arita amounts to 1174, with 5430 inhabitants; 120 houses are engaged in porcelain-making, 30 in porcelain-painting, and there are some 1560 workmen. The company employs not less than 450 potters and painters, many of them skilled hands, and there is every reason to believe that it will shortly be advanced to a prosperous situation.

The village of Okawaji-mura lies three miles in a northerly direction from Arita, whither the works were removed about A.D. 1710 by Prince Nabeshima from Iwayagawa, near Arita, the latter place being in proximity to a public highway, and not suitable for the secrecy required. The works at Okawaji-mura were under the local government of the prince, and the produce consisted solely of the best kind of ware, such as plates, tea cups, and ornamental pieces used as offerings to the Imperial Court and the Shogun, or to supply the demand of various princes. Its private sale was positively prohibited. (Nos. 189-196.) The lower edge of the saucers for the cups is painted in blue colour with a design resembling the teeth of a comb, distinguishing it as official work, hence it obtained the name of *Kushité*, meaning the ware with comb-teeth. It is very much appreciated by the public. (Nos. 190, 193, and 194.) Two varieties of Celadon were also produced, one being an imitation of the Chinese

Fig. 57.
Kushité pattern.

(No. 192), and the other a peculiar kind finely crackled. The latter is much admired by the people. At present, through the want of good workmen, no fine pieces can be obtained. The Koransha of Arita is, however, making great efforts to restore the ancient tradition. (No. 197.)

The works of Shida, Koshida, and Yoshida are situated together in a village not far from Ureshino in the province of Hizen. These factories were severally established in the period Meiwa (1764–71), and manufactured articles for domestic use ornamented with cobalt, coloured enamels not being employed. Plates only were produced at the Shida works, while both at Koshida and Yoshida cheap and inferior tea cups and bowls for eating formed part of the trade. The greater part of the material came from the vicinity of the works, but it was mixed with a clay from Amakusa Island.

The factory at Matsugaya was built in the earlier part of the period Kiyoho (A.D. 1716–35), by direction of a branch of the Nabeshima family, who obtained a maker from Arita to carry on the trade. The porcelain made at these works is very excellent, and to some extent resembles the Okawaji ware, but it is never painted. The factory was closed some fifty years ago, consequently its produce has become very scarce. It is said that Celadon was made there, but no specimen is known.

### SHONSUI WARE.

165. DISH (*sara*), with upright edge ; porcelain, painted in blue with
     flying birds, detached sprigs, and symbols ; border of geometrical
     diaper ; outside, border of scrolls ; bottom unglazed.  Made by
     Gorodayiu Go Shonsui about 1580–90.  Diam. 9 in.    323.77.
     We give here the date of the Japanese Report ; but if Gorodayiu
     Go Shonsiu returned from China in 1513, he must have been a very
     old man in 1580 or 1590.
166. CYLINDRICAL CUP; porcelain, painted in blue ; outside round the
     lip are five panels with diapers and landscapes, below which are
     vertical flutes, alternately two in blue and one in white ; inside
     a border of panels, each with a figure on a monster.  Mark in
     a square, *Fuku*, " Happiness."  [Similar to figure 50.]  Made
     by Gorodayiu Go Shonsui, 1580–90.  H. 2⅞ in.      324.77.

### ARITA WARE.

167. ORNAMENT (*oki-mono*), in the form of a youth standing ; por-
     celain, slightly painted in red, green, and blue ; among the
     ornaments occurs the character *Jiu*, " Longevity."  His right
     hand is placed in his breast.  Made at Arita, province of Hizen,
     about 1650.  H. 12½ in.                           325.77.
168. PAIR OF BEAKERS, octagonal at the mouth ; porcelain, painted
     in colours with gilding ; shaped panels with diapers, land-
     scapes, etc., irregularly disposed on a ground of peonies with
     blue leaves ; round the lips a double band of panels enclosing
     diapers, chrysanthemums, etc.  Made at Arita, province of
     Hizen, about 1670.  H. 23¼ in. diam. 10½ in.      326.77.
169. OVIFORM VASE AND COVER ; porcelain, richly painted in colours
     with gilding ; panels of various shapes, trefoil, etc., containing
     female figures and flowers.  The cover has been strengthened
     and mounted with gilt and silvered metal.  Ebony stand.  Made
     at Arita about 1690.  H. 34¼ in. diam. 16½ in.    327.77.
170. INCENSE BURNER (*koro*), of porcelain, with a globular body, rest-
     ing on three legs, and a pierced cover surmounted by a monster ;
     on it various ornaments in low relief, painted in brilliant colours,
     red, green, and pale blue, with gilding ; on the body three quatre-
     foil panels with flowers on a bright red ground ; between them,
     hares on waves ; on the cover dragons.  Made at Arita about
     1710.  H. 7¾ in. diam. 4¾ in.  [Figure 58.]      328.77.
171. INCENSE BURNER (*koro*), in the form of a cock crowing ; the head

and neck forming a cover so that the smoke would issue from the mouth ; porcelain, enamelled in the natural colours with gilding. Made at Arita about 1740. H. 9½ in. l. 7¼ in.

329.77.

Fig. 58. Incense Burner. Arita ware. No. 170.

172. LARGE DISH (*sara*); porcelain, painted in red and blackish blue ; in the centre a vase of peonies ; border of trees, prunus, etc., with cloud-like panels in red. Made at Arita about 1740. Diam. 22¼ in. 330.77.

173. LARGE DISH (*sara*); porcelain, painted in red and blackish blue,
with touches of green and gilding ; in the centre two storks,
with prunus, bamboo, etc. ; border of trellis-work, divided into
three parts, each containing a quatrefoil panel with a phœnix.
Made at Arita about 1740.  Diam. 21 in.        331.77.

174. SQUARE SAKÉ BOTTLE (*saké-iré*), the body tapering towards the
base, the shoulders truncated ; a very small neck ; porcelain,
painted in colours with gilding ; panels of irregular form containing chrysanthemums and other flowers, with patches of

Fig. 59.  Arita.  No. 177.

diaper as a ground ; on the shoulders diapers.  Made at Arita,
about 1770.  H. 7⅜ in.        332.77.

175. PLATE (*sara*), with shaped edge ; porcelain, painted in colours
with gilding ; in the centre an irregular panel, with a three-
clawed dragon ; on the edge two long panels, each with a bird
on a rock ; the ground dull blue with white scrolls outlined in
gold, and with red flowers, etc., scattered over the surface.
Made at Arita, about 1790.  Diam. 9⅜ in.        333.77.

176. SAUCER DISH (*sara*) ; porcelain, painted in enamel colours with
peonies, in citron, green, white, and red, with liver-coloured
leaves, on a greenish ground.  Made at Arita, about 1790.  Diam.
18½ in.        334.77.

177. BOWL (*hachi*) ; porcelain, richly painted in colours, with gilding ;

inside, in the centre, an European ship; round this a band of lozenge diaper in green and purple, on it two panels with European ships and two with imitations of European shields; between them pairs of European men in eighteenth century costume; outside, two medallions with ships and two with figures, with peonies between them. Mark in gold *Jiu,* "Longevity." [Figure 59.] Made at Arita, about 1800. H. 3½ in. diam. 10 in. 335.77.

178. PAIR OF SAKÉ JUGS (*saké-ire*), with pear-shaped bodies and narrow necks; porcelain, painted in blue and red with gilding; on each side a shaped panel with flowers, surrounded by trees in bloom. Made at Arita, about 1810. H. 6⅛ in.

336. 336A.77.

179. TWO CUPS AND SAUCERS; porcelain, painted in colours with gilding; on the cups, two medallions with flowers; between, diapers, etc., in red, with symbols; on saucers, trefoil conventional design in red, blue, etc. Mark of the Chinese period Ching-hwa, 1465–1488. [Figure 60.] Made at Arita, about 1810. H. of cup 2⅜ in. diam. 3⅝ in., diam. of saucer 5¼ in. 337.77.

大 化
明 年
成 製

Fig. 60.
Arita.
No. 179.

Fig. 61.
Arita.
No. 180.

180. DISH (*sara*), in the form of a haliotis shell (*awabi*); porcelain, painted in brilliant colours, with touches of gilding; flowers in circles, etc., scattered over the surface, and patches of diaper in panels of the form of conventional Japanese clouds. Mark in a square, *Fuku,* "Happiness." [Figure 61.] Made at Arita, about 1820. L. 10⅜ in. 338.77.

181. BOWL (*hachi*), fluted in sixteen lobes, with scalloped edge; porcelain, painted in brilliant colours, with gilding; inside in the centre a formal chrysanthemum of sixteen petals; the ornament around this fills alternately one and two lobes, the former diapers, the latter with scrolls and chrysanthemums; the outside diapered with quatrefoils and red discs. Mark of the Chinese period Ching-hwa, 1465–1488. [Figure 60.] Made at Arita, about 1840. H. 2¾ in. diam. 8 in. 339.77.

182. TWO SAUCER DISHES (*sara*), with shaped edges; porcelain, painted in colours with gilding. Inside in the centre a medallion surrounded by lozenge diaper in red and green, and three

heart-shaped panels with scrolls, on a red ground ; at the back blue scrolls. Mark of the Chinese period Ching-hwa, 1465–1488. [Figure 60.] Made at Arita, about 1840. Diam. 7 in.

340.77.

大
日
本
皿 肥
山 前
深
川
製

Fig. 62.
Arita.
No. 183.

183. LARGE DISH (*sara*) ; porcelain, delicately painted in rich colours with gilding ; prunus trees, peonies, birds, etc. ; outside ornamented in blue, with birds and seaweed. Mark in red on gold and blue, *Dai Ni-pon Hi-zen Sara-yama Fuka-gawa sei*, "Made by Fukagawa at Sarayama, Hizen, in Great Japan." [Figure 62.] Made by Yeizayemon Fukagawa, at Arita, 1875. Diam. 36 in. 341.77.

184. FLOWER VASE (*hana-ike*) ; porcelain, with a bluish grey glaze, painted with an archaic pattern in colours with gilding ; the body covered with slender plants with narrow red and yellow leaves ; on the shoulder a band of running scroll on red ground ; round the body a white band, on which a conventional bird, alternating with four *tamas* in flames, all among clouds ; border at foot of two alternate diapers. Mark in red, *Fuka-mi sei*, "Made by Fukami." [Figure 63.] Made by Suminosuké Fukami, at Arita, 1875. H. 11¼ in. 342.77.

185. PAIR OF FLOWER VASES (*hana-ike*), pear-shaped and slightly ribbed, copied in design from an ancient bronze ; porcelain, covered with a pale primrose glaze ; from the base proceed leaf-shaped points of diaper ; round the neck a dragon in relief. Mark, *Fuka sei*, "Made by Fuka." Made by Suminosuké Fukami, at Arita, 1875. H. 6¼ in. 343.77.

老

三 辻 肥

製 製 前

Fig. 63.    Fig. 64.
Arita.    Arita.
No. 184.    No. 186.

186. COFFEE POT, of European form, with the handle and lining of cover pierced ; delicate porcelain, painted in black, green, and red with gilding ; on the body groups of fern in black and gold ; delicate borders in gold, etc. Mark, in gold, *Hi-zen Tsuji sei*, "Made by [Katsuzô] Tsuji, in Hizen." [Figure 64.] Made at Arita, 1875. H. 5⅝ in.

344.77.

187. SUCRIER, with two pierced handles and revolving knob to cover ; *en suite* with the last, similarly decorated and with the same mark. H. 3⅝ in. diam. 5¼ in. 345.77.

OKAWAJI WARE.

188. QUADRANGULAR INCENSE BURNER (*koro*), consisting of a tray with four feet, supporting a trough, over which fits a cover of pierced network ; at the sides are alternately a tree and a *koi* fish at a waterfall ; borders of leaves and cinquefoils on a red ground. Made at Okawaji, province of Hizen, about 1740. H. 5¾ in. L. 5⅜ in. 346.77.

189. TWO SHAPED DISHES (*sara*), in the form of an armorial badge ; the design is known as the *daki-botan*, and represents a peony flower, with a branch of leaves on each side, as if embracing it. Made at Okawaji, about 1770. L. 6⅝ in. 347.77.

190. SAUCER DISH (*sara*), porcelain ; painted in green and blue ; inside, fern-like branches and other leaves ; outside, scrolls in blue, and comb teeth (*kushité*) border to foot-rim. [Figure 57.] Made at Okawaji, about 1770. Diam. 4½ in. 348.77.

191. INCENSE BURNER (*koro*) and cover, in the form of a low vase with part of the ornament in very low relief, the cover surmounted by the figure of an old man seated, covered with a celadon glaze ; porcelain, painted in colours with gilding ; on the body a boy climbing a pine tree ; and a three-clawed dragon among clouds near a prunus tree ; scattered about are seal characters signifying the sun, the autumn moon, and spring. Made at Okawaji, about 1770. H. 7⅛ in. 349.77.

192. QUADRANGULAR INCENSE BURNER (*koro*), in the form of a two-handled vase, with ornaments in relief and on the cover a seated figure of Fukurokujiu, the god of Longevity ; buff porcelain, covered with a celadon glaze, the head, feet, and hand of the figure left unglazed. Made at Okawaji, about 1770. H. 6⅛ in. diam. 4¾ in. 350.77.

193. SAUCER DISH (*sara*) ; porcelain, painted in blue and other colours ; inside, a basket with high handle, containing fruit and flowers ; comb-teeth border to foot-rim. Made at Okawaji, about 1810. Diam. 8 in. 351.77.

194. SAUCER DISH (*sara*) ; porcelain, painted in blue, red, and green ; inside, azaleas and magnolia ; outside, patches of flowers and comb-teeth border to foot-rim. Made at Okawaji, about 1810. Diam. 8 in. 352.77.

195. INCENSE BURNER (*koro*), with pierced cover, of pear-shaped form, resting on a flattened sphere ; porcelain, with dark-blue decoration, formal plants, etc. Made at Okawaji, about 1810. H. 6½ in. diam. 3⅛ in. 353.77.

196. PEN REST (*hikka*), in the form of a branch of prunus tree in bloom ; porcelain, painted in the natural colours. Made at Okawaji, about 1820.  L. 4⅛ in.   354.77.

深 日
川 肥
製 山

Fig. 65.
Okawaji.
No. 197.

197. PAIR OF FLOWER VASES (*hana-ike*) ; celadon porcelain, crackled ; the body of each is richly ornamented in brilliant enamel colours with gilding, with five-petalled flowers and leaves ; round the neck storks among clouds on red ground ; round the base a band of green scale work with conventional waves and two sacred tortoises.  Mark, *Nichi Hi-zen Fuka-gawa sei,* " Made by Fukagawa of Nichi Hizen."  [Figure 65.] Made at Okawaji, 1875.                      355.77.

## SHIRA-ISHI WARE.

Very little is known of the origin of this ware.  It is, however, a fact that it has developed most remarkably and has even been exported since the advent, twenty years ago, of a porcelain-maker of Kiôto, named Sowa.  The materials are found in the neighbourhood, but are mixed with a clay from the Island of Amakusa. The ware made here is perfectly white and covered with a network of crackles, and the ornamentation is excellently executed with vitreous substances.  The crackled Celadon is somewhat darker than the Okawaji ware.

[There is no specimen of this ware in the collection.]

## MIKAWAJI WARE.

Mikawaji is situated in the county of Matsu-ura, six miles distant in a southerly direction from Arita.  The works were established in the period Meireki (about A.D. 1655–57), by a man named Imamura Sannojo and his son, descendants of a Corean, in accordance with the order of a prince of the Matsu-ura family residing at Hirato.  Hence the articles made here are generally called *Hirato ware,* and are either for the use of the prince, or as presents to the Shogun, or to others from him.  The Sometsuké painted with Chinese boys playing under a pine tree were especially for the use of the prince, and their sale was prohibited. (Nos. 198 and 202.)

The value of the ware varies according to the number of boys painted on it. The best has seven boys, the next five, and the ordinary ware only three. In consequence of its scarcity it is in great demand, and any person who has the good fortune to obtain a piece, at once procures a case for its protection. Another description of porcelain manufactured here is ornamented with designs in relief, produced by engraving, and also by tracing with a brush dipped in thin clay pulp, prepared by mixing the clay with water. (No. 203.) These productions are, on account of their good workmanship, considered as masterpieces, and cannot be made at any other factory.

Mr. Fukami Suminosuké, a distinguished porcelain-maker of Arita, with whom we visited the works last year, was much struck with them, and resolved that the art should on no account be allowed to become extinct. Consequently, on his return to Arita he turned his attention to the production of this ware, and made a pair of flower vases, which were exhibited at the Philadelphia Exhibition. In the period Tempo, in 1837, a potter named Ikeda Yasujiro made a very thin paper-like and glossy translucent porcelain known as egg-shell. Small pieces only were made, turned on the potter's wheel. In later years it has been painted with enamel of various colours, and largely exported. The material used comes from the Island of Amakusa, or Goto, and is softer and tougher than that from Idsumi-yama. (No. 204.)

198. TWO SAUCER DISHES (*sara*); porcelain, painted in greyish blue ; five Chinese boys catching butterflies under a pine tree ; scallop borders ; no foot-rim, bottom unglazed. Made at Mikawaji, about 1770. Diam. 5⅜ in.                          356.77.
199. CYLINDRICAL FLOWER VASE (*hana-ike*) ; ornamented with five bands of raised circular medallions ; porcelain, painted in blue ; a symbol or diaper on each medallion. Made at Mikawaji, about 1790. H. 7½ in. diam. 4⅜ in.              357.77.

H

200. ORNAMENT (*oki-mono*), in the form of a conventional lion, standing on a rock, from which spring peonies in white biscuit ; porcelain, painted in blue and brown.  Made at Mikawaji, about
1790.  H. 8¼ in.  [Figure 66.]  358.77.

201. SAKÉ JUG (*saké-ire*), in the form of a fat man seated, and with a
large bag behind him, the neck of which rests on his right
shoulder and forms a spout ; porcelain, with various glazes, the

Fig. 66.  Lion.  Mikawaji ware.  No. 200.

bag being yellow, the man's cloak blue ; cover wanting.  Made
at Mikawaji, about 1800.  H. 5¼ in. l. 7¼ in.  359.77.

202. TWO GLOBULAR INCENSE BURNERS (*koro*), with pierced trellis
covers ; porcelain, painted in blue ; on each five Chinese boys
at play, and fir trees.  Made at Mikawaji, about 1830. H. 2¾ in.
diam. 3½ in.  360.77.

203. FLOWER VASE (*hana-ike*), with two handles, globular body and
small foot ; porcelain, painted in enamel colours with gilding ;
on one side a quatrefoil in biscuit, on which, in slight relief, a
conventional lion among waves and clouds ; on the other side
the *sho chiku bai*, viz. fir, prunus, and bamboo trees ; on the neck

phœnixes on gold ground. Two marks : 1. Impressed, and forming a ring round the base, *Dai Ni-pon Mi-kawa-ji sei*, " Made at Mikawaji in Great Japan."

2. In red, *Oité Ko-ran-sha Sei-zan sei*," Made by Seizan at the Koransha." [Figure 67.] Made 1875. H. 6½ in. 361.77.

204. TEA CUP WITH HANDLE AND SAUCER, of European form ; egg-shell porcelain, painted in red with gilding ; on each are six oblong white panels, each containing a figure of a poet ; red ground with comb-like objects in gold. Mark, *Mi-kawa-ji Mori Chikara tsukuru*, " Made by Mori Chikara, at Mikawaji." [Figure 68.] 1875. Cup h. 2½ in. diam. 2⅞ in., saucer diam. 5¼ in. 362.77.

大 日 本 三 河 森 三  
於 香 蘭 內 力 川  
西 山 社 製 造 內  
製 製

Fig. 67. Mikawaji. No. 203.

Fig. 68. Mikawaji. No. 204.

### KAMEYAMA WARE.

This kiln is situated on a hill near Nagasaki. The date of its foundation is not known. It is certain, however, that it was established after the Arita system, for the purpose of imitating the Chinese Sometsuké, by making use of a clay found on the Island of Amakusa. Since the period Tempo (A.D. 1830–43) a material has been imported from China, and is employed mostly in the manufacture of tea services or saké vessels. They are grey in colour, of a coarse body, painted with dark-blue colour, resembling a kind of Chinese porcelain known as *Gosu*. This ware met with great favour from amateurs until within the last ten years ; since then the quality of the ware has declined, and the factory is now closed.

[The specimen of this ware is no longer in the collection, having been lost or broken before it reached England.]

### SANDA WARE.

The kiln from which this ware emanated was erected in the period Genroku (A.D. 1688-1703), on the Arita principle, by the Prince of Setsu, of the Kuki family, who were princes under the old feudal system now abolished. The factory was started for the purpose of imitating the Chinese Celadon, which ranked high in the public favour. Great success attended the enterprise, and an experienced man can scarcely distinguish the imitation from the original, or even from the ancient Japanese Celadon, which was also a reproduction of the Chinese ware. Sanda Celadon is much appreciated ; but the works have declined, and only an inferior porcelain used by the neighbouring farmers is now made.

205. INCENSE BURNER (*koro*), in the form of a cock looking back-
wards ; porcelain, covered with celadon glaze. Sanda ware,
made about 1710.  H. 8¾ in. l. 8¾ in.               363.77.

206. INCENSE BURNER (*koro*), in the shape of an oviform cage, pierced
in trellis pattern, and resting on a flat tripod base ; porcelain,
covered with a celadon glaze. Sanda ware, made in 1767.
H. 9¼ in.                                           364.77.

### TOZAN WARE.

This ware is from a private factory in the town of Himeji, in the province of Harima, founded by the family of Sakai (formerly princes under the feudal system), for the purpose of imitating the Arita ware. Dinner and tea services, so-called *Migakité*, have been made after the Chinese *Somet-suké* of the Middle Ages, and the Celadon produced here is somewhat finer than that known as Nankin Celadon in China. For the last fifteen years the works have been degenerating, and at present only a small trade in inferior wares is carried on.

姫
路
製
Fig. 69.
Tozan.
No. 207.

207. PAIR OF PRICKET CANDLESTICKS (*shoku-dai*), with
bowl-shaped nozzles, mounted in wood and copper, below which
cylindrical stems, resting on saucer-shaped bowls ; tall bell-
shaped bases ; porcelain, painted in blue ; on the stems, sym-

bols ; on the bases, landscapes. Mark, *Hime-ji sei,* "Made at
Himeji." [Figure 69.] Tozan ware, made about 1820. H. 15¾ in.
                                                                365.77.
208. OVIFORM FLOWER VASE (*hana-ike*), with two fixed handles, in.
the form of three interlacing rings ; porcelain, covered with a
very light celadon glaze, much paler at the angles. Tozan ware,
made about 1820.  H. 8⅝ in.                                     366.77.

## ŌTA WARE.

The kiln at Ōta, near Yokohama, was established after the
opening of the harbour, by a merchant named Suzuki Yasubei,
for the purpose of manufacturing an imitation of the Satsuma
ware, the materials being procured from the province of Satsuma.
He brought over a Kiyomidzu porcelain-maker named Kozan,
who was living at Makudsu-ga-hara, in Kiôto, and who worked
with such success that the original Satsuma ware lost its value.
Kozan had been long waiting for an opportunity of displaying his
ability, and applied last year to the Philadelphia Commission to
obtain leave to show his work at the Philadelphia Exhibition.
His application was accepted, and, he being a poor man, money
was advanced to him.  With this encouragement he succeeded in
producing some very creditable specimens of his work, which
have been much admired by the public visiting the Exhibition.
He is still a young man, and there is every reason to believe that
he will improve.

[It is from this manufactory, as well as from the Awata factory
near Kiôto, that has issued the great quantity of pottery commonly
sold as Satsuma ware.]

209. PAIR OF OVIFORM VASES AND COVERS, the surface imitating
basket-work ; grey ware, glazed, and richly painted in colours
with flowering plants ; on the shoulders the armorial badge of
the Tokugawa family (see Introduction, p. 18), formerly Shoguns
of Japan, three times repeated ; the covers surmounted by
figures of two conventional lions fighting.  Made at Ōta, in
1869, in imitation of old Satsuma ware.  H. 30 in.     368.77.

### ADDITIONAL SPECIMENS.

210. PAIR OF FLOWER VASES (*hana-ike*), with shaped handles ; porcelain, painted in colours with gilding ; on the body of each, four
fishes and a tortoise swimming ; on the
shoulder a band of rich diaper with
quatrefoils ; small borders at neck and
foot ; on neck two birds in gold. Marks :
1. Blue under glaze, *Hi-zen Tsuji sei*,
"Made by Tsuji in Hizen." 2. In red, *Ni-
pon To-kiyo Hyo-chi-yen gua*, "Painted
at the Hyochiyen of Tokio, Japan."
[Figure 70.] Arita ware, decorated at
Tokio in 1875. H. 8⅜ in.    367.77.

瓢 日
池 本 幹
園 東 山
口 京 製

Fig. 70.    Fig. 71.
Arita.     Kiyomidzu.
No. 210.   No. 211.

211. PAIR OF FLOWER VASES (*hana-ike*), with
oviform bodies and shaped handles ;
porcelain, richly painted in colours with
gilding ; on each are two panels with
flowers ; ground of key pattern in gold on red ; on the necks
phœnixes among clouds ; on the bases, diapers. Mark, *Kanzan sei*, "Made by Kanzan." [Figure 71.] Made at Kiyomidzu,
by Kanzan Denshichi in 1875. H. 14½ in.    369.77.

212. PAIR OF FLOWER VASES (*hana-ike*), with long oviform bodies ;
porcelain, covered with raised outlines representing a prunus
tree in bloom. Mark, *Dai Ni-pon
Sei-fu tsukuru*, "Made by Seifu of
Great Japan." [Figure 72.] Made at
Kiyomidzu in 1875.    370.77.

清 大 道 大
風 日 八 日
造 本 製 本

Fig. 72.      Fig. 73.
Kiyomidzu.    Kiyomidzu.
No. 212.      No. 213.

213. PAIR OF FLOWER VASES (*hana-ike*) ;
chocolate-glazed ware imitating basket-
work, with twigs forming handles.
Mark scratched, *Dai Ni-pon Dô-hachi
sei*, "Made by Dôhachi, Great Japan."
Made at Kiyomidzu, by Takahashi
Dôhachi, 1875. H. 12⅜ in. 371.77.

214. FLOWER POT (*hana-hachi*), of European form ; porcelain, the
outside with red ground and inscriptions in white, of twenty-nine
lines, being a passage from a work by Wang Hi-che, a Chinese
prose writer, who lived A.D. 321–379 ; two gilt borders. Made by
Takahashi Dôhachi, at Kiyomidzu, 1875. H. 6⅜ in.   372.77.

215. TEA POT (*do-bin*), with overarching handle ; thin grey ware with
    pitted surface, with an incised inscription, consisting of Japanese
    verses ; the lid in the shape of a nelumbium leaf. Made at Kiôto
    by the nun Rengetsu, in 1867.   H. 5⅝ in.            373.77.
216. PAN (*suri-hachi*), for washing rice ; coarse red ware, covered with
    a reddish-brown glaze, the inside rough with radiating comb
    marks.   Japanese.   No locality.   Diam. 12¾ in.      374.77.

BADGE OF THE PRINCE OF SOMA.

# LIST OF POTTERS AND DECORATORS

## WHO EXHIBITED AT THE PARIS EXHIBITION, 1878.

*₊* In Japan the family name is usually followed by the personal name.  In order, however, to conform with European usage, the names were transposed in the catalogue of the Paris Exhibition, 1878, and the personal and more important name reduced to an initial.  In this list the defect has been remedied ; and by omitting the commas the names will be found to be placed as they are in the Report.  The names with an asterisk are those of decorators *only*.

| NAMES. | PLACES. | PROVINCES. |
|---|---|---|
| Abé, Ômi. | Kanazawa. | Kaga. |
| *Akiyama, Teiji. | Nagoya. | Owari. |
| *Aoki, Torakichi. | Tokio. | |
| Asano, Zihei. | Nagoya. | Owari. |
| Daté, Denzaburo. | Hamaishiki. | Isé. |
| Daté, Kasuké. | Suenaga. | do. |
| Hara, Huzio. | Nagoya. | Owari. |
| *Hattori, Kiôho. | Tokio. | |
| Hattori, Tsuna. | do. | |
| *Higuchi, Yasukichi. | do. | |
| Hori, Tomonao. | Higashi-akuragawa. | Isé. |
| *Hujishima, Sentarô. | Nagoya. | Owari. |
| *Hyochiyen Company. | Tokio. | |
| Iriyama, Kainosuké. | Yokkaichi. | Isé. |
| Ishima, Sasuké. | do. | do. |
| Ito, Hanzô. | do. | do. |
| Ito, Kichibei. | do. | do. |
| Iwata, Suzukichi. | Nagoya. | Owari. |
| Kanzan, Denshichi. | Kiôto. | |
| Kato, Gosuké. | Ichinokura. | Mino |

| NAMES. | PLACES. | PROVINCES. |
|---|---|---|
| Kato, Kansiro. | Seto. | Owari |
| Kato, Kichibei. | do. | do. |
| Kato, Magoyémon. | do. | do. |
| Kato, Mokuzayémon. | do. | do. |
| Kato, Monzayémon. | do. | do. |
| Kato, Shuhei. | do. | do. |
| Kato, Shigehirô. | do. | do. |
| Kawamoto, Hansuké. | do. | do. |
| Kawamoto, Masakichi. | do. | do. |
| Kawamoto, Rikichi. | do. | do. |
| Ki-ima, Yei (a lady). | Kiôto. | |
| Kinkozan, Sobei. | do. | |
| Kobayashi, Masakichi. | Yokkaichi. | Isé. |
| Kôno, Taiga. | Akasaka. | Mino. |
| Kôransha Company. | Arita. | Hizen. |
| Marunaka, Magohei. | Kanazawa. | Kaga. |
| *Matsumoto, Yoshinobu. | Tokio. | |
| Miyagawa, Kôzan. | Ota, near Yokohama. | Musashi. |
| Miyai, Sajurô. | Otamura. | Kishiu. |
| Mori, Shokichi. | Hamaishiki. | Isé. |
| Mori, Yogozayémon. | Yokkaichi. | do. |
| Murayama, Kôshiro. | Hamaishiki. | do. |
| Nagaya, Yôzô. | Hiogo. | Settsu. |
| Nakayama, Magoshichi. | Yokkaichi. | Isé. |
| Naruse, Waroku. | Tokio. | |
| Oki, Toyosuké. | Nagoya. | Owari. |
| Ota, Jiuyemon. | Hamaishiki. | Isé. |
| Ota, Mankichi. | Imadomura. | Tokio. |
| Sakata, Kikuzirô. | do. | do. |
| Sasada, Kurazi. | Kanazawa. | Kaga. |
| Satô, Kumezô. | Yokkaichi. | Isé. |
| Seifu, Yohei. | Kiôto. | |
| Shippo Kuaisha Company. | Seto. | Owari. |
| Shigetomi, Heizo. | Yokkaichi. | Isé. |
| Shimidzu, Kichibei. | Kiôto. | |

| NAMES. | PLACES. | PROVINCES. |
|---|---|---|
| Shimidzu, Onko. | Akasaka. | Mino. |
| Shimidzu, Rokubei. | Kiôto. | |
| Shimidzu, Sekisen. | Akasaka. | Mino. |
| Shitomi, Shohei. | Hamaishiki. | Isé. |
| Takagi, Tansai. | Yokkaichi. | do. |
| Takahashi, Dôhachi. | Kiôto. | |
| Takaoka, Guenzô. | Hiogo. | Settsu. |
| Takasu, Kitchijuro. | Toyohashi. | Mikawa. |
| Takemoto, Hayata. | Tokio. | |
| Tani, Sumi. | Hamaishiki. | Isé. |
| Tanzan, Seikai. | Kiôto. | |
| Tsukada, Kiyomatsu. | Hamaishiki. | Isé. |
| Uchimoto, Koichirô. | Kiôto. | |
| Waké, Kitei. | do. | |
| *Yamada, Mohichi. | Nagoya. | Owari. |
| Yamamoto, Kazuma. | Yokkaichi. | Isé. |
| Yamamoto, Matasaburo. | Yokohama. | Musashi. |
| Yamanaka, Chiuzayémon. | Suenaga. | Isé. |
| Yeiraku, Zengorô. | Kiôto. | |
| Yeiraku, Zenichirô. | Toyohashi. | Mikawa. |
| Yeisinsha. | Idzushi. | Tazima. |
| Yokoï, Sôsuké. | Nagoya. | Owari. |
| Yota, Makita. | Idzushi. | Tajima. |

HAMMER OF DAIKOKU. (From a native woodcut.

# INDEX.

www.ingramcontent.com/pod-product-compliance
Lightning Source LLC
Chambersburg PA
CBHW030618270326
41927CB00007B/1220